READING FOR THE LONG RUN

Reading for the Long Run

Leading Struggling Students into the Reading Life

Sara Osborne

Foreword by Cheryl Swope

CiRCE
Concord, NC

Published in the USA
by the CiRCE Institute
© 2023 Sara Osborne

ISBN 979-8-9869172-4-5

For information:
CiRCE Institute
81 McCachern Blvd
Concord, NC 28025s
www.circeinstitute.com

For the parents and teachers of struggling readers—
may you be reminded of the worthiness of your occupation.

Contents

Foreword

Sara Osborne is a runner. With focus and determination, she knows how to train, grapple with setbacks, accept coaching, and persevere. Sara is also a teacher, a mother, and an advocate of classical Christian education. We meet the intersection of these roles in her book, but this is more than a memoir. This book is intended to serve as a companion and a guide.

When one of Sara's children struggled with reading, Sara fought to find a way to teach him to read. Initial strategies and efforts did not produce the results she desired. In her book, she shares openly that when difficulties ensued, her questions grew. *How can I help my son when I do not know how to teach a child with learning difficulties? Where do I find help?*

An avid reader and unafraid of thinking deeply, Sara began to ask broader questions. *Is this immense undertaking worth it? If yes, why? Why do we learn to read? How will a classical education remain beneficial for my struggling reader?* Sara began asking herself additional questions with "acute honesty." *Is learning to read really a necessity for a child with daunting challenges? Why are you making this such a priority? Do you want this for him or for yourself?*

In *Reading for the Long Run*, the author shares her experiences and reflections in a thought-provoking collection of insight, practical tips, and application. With an overarching metaphor, Sara applies principles gleaned from years of running. Rest assured, this is no trite proclamation that teaching is a marathon, not a sprint; rather, Sara's book highlights preparation, disciplined habits, the marking of milestones, the prevention of injuries, and encouragement for staying the course.

Sara's contributions to this book are not limited to her own experiences. She draws wisely from those who have inspired her to consider the benefits of giving a struggling learner an excellent education. Through this book, she shares much of what is needed to teach a child with learning difficulties.

She says that the adults in his life must first identify what the student needs and then provide it. As if with a wide lens, Sara shares a vision beyond mere reading instruction, though this will be necessary. Specialized reading lessons, such as those designed within Orton-Gillingham, Wilson, Barton, Simply Classical, and other programs, may be needed. Additionally for the classical student, instruction may require a trained tutor or reading specialist willing to teach in a manner consistent with classical education in philosophy and pedagogy. Support may include ancillary therapies, improved nutrition, prescribed exercise, intentional teaching of discernment with screens, and plenty of coaching. Sara shares from experience that we must indeed continue coaching the child long after he takes his first steps.

Sara claims neither to be an expert in reading nor a trained teacher of reading. Instead, throughout the book Sara interviews and quotes others. She interviews her son's practitioner to share the practical suggestions and support that benefited her family. Sara draws from writings and research on dyslexia, cognitive science, and reading instruction. Given her background in classical education, she expertly weaves together the thoughts of Frederick Douglass, C. S. Lewis, and Cheryl Lowe of Memoria Press.

In one of numerous highlights, Sara shares an interview from Dr. Kevin Clark, an author and leader in classical education. As the founder of an initiative devoted to bringing a classical education to students with a broad range of innate abilities, Dr. Clark lends much wisdom to the conversation. Sara's intent is to place all of her thoughts within the greater context of classical Christian education.

From Sara's conversation with Dr. Clark, we receive encouragement for all of our children. He shares that in his school, "some of our students have a unique configuration of challenges that make reading difficult: dyslexia, dysgraphia, and ADHD. Yet we require all of our students to build up the habit of reading each night." We learn that he allows and encourages the use of audio books at times, such as when higher-level works surpass a student's current reading ability. Dr. Clark assures us that "by listening and following along, students necessarily build up the habits of attention and endurance and stamina."

In his conversation with Sara, Dr. Clark makes this key observation:

> There will be different depths to which people master the arts of grammar or logic or rhetoric, but if those . . . are truly liberating— if they set you free with respect to language so that you're not at the mercy of language but can use it wisely and well for loving your neighbor and loving the truth—then everyone needs that kind of learning.

He says that reading is "a task which requires an active imagination," but he asserts, "It isn't that people either have imagination or don't. It's something trained in us." He says, "The more you read, the more you hone the ability to see the world the way the author is describing it."

While talking with Sara, Dr. Clark explains that when students read, they begin to "learn how to enter into a text, to follow a line of thought that an author is developing." He notes that this enables the child to see better the point of view of people in their own lives. He tells Sara that reading expands our capacity to understand more and to experience more. The premise is simple: "The posture necessary for reading is receptive, and it's patient. There is a baseline of humility."

Similarly, the humility and earnestness with which Sara approaches her conversations is noteworthy. As we read this book, we sense that this is something Sara has felt compelled to write. She has learned through her dear son's challenges and feels duty-bound to impart the knowledge she has gained along the way.

Sara's sincerity pervades these observations. *My frustration and rush leads him to bristle and worry; conversely, my focus and calm call him to attentiveness and growth.* Her God-given, hard-won humility draws us closer to her message, as she shares truth: *In God's good providence, loving another person ends up not only affecting him—but also changing me for the better.* We find ourselves cheering for Sara and for her son. We find ourselves wanting all children to learn to read—and, just as importantly, for all of us to read more.

In this book we hear words from C. S. Lewis in *An Experiment in Criticism*: "Those of us who have been true readers all our lives seldom realize the enormous extension of our being which we owe to authors ... [We read to] see with other eyes, to feel with other hearts."[1] In other words, reading is no mere skill. Sara adds this from Vigen Guroian, "Stories are an irreplaceable medium for this kind of moral education—that is, the education of character."[2] As Sara reminds us, "One of the most significant gifts you can give your struggling reader is to fill her mind with rich, engaging sentences and stories."

When reading *Reading for the Long Run*, we come to believe that the very discipline of learning to read may support character formation.

1. C.S. Lewis, *An Experiment in Criticism*, (Cambridge: University Press, 1961), 137.

2. Vigen Guroian, *Tending the Heart of Virtue: How Classic Stories Awaken a Child's Moral Imagination* (New York: Oxford University Press, 1998), 20.

Sara observes that in the "years engaged in focused reading remediation and visual skill building, my struggling student has grown in determination, discipline, fortitude, and independence." It is no surprise that, as a dedicated runner, mother, and educator, Sara believes, "Yes, teaching my child to read is worth the effort, the energy, the time, the struggle— for him and for me." She adds, "Sometimes I feel this truth in the depths of my soul. Sometimes I preach it to myself through choked-back tears: *a reading life may be one of the greatest gifts I give my children.*"

A surprising benefit of this book is that in her maternal quest to explore reading instruction, reading struggles, and the reading life, Sara reminds us that one of the greatest gifts we can give ourselves is to begin or to continue reading deeply, even as we seek to bestow the benefits of reading to our children. When we read a good book deeply, we teach children by example that reading a good book is a high calling worthy of our time. We can freely eschew tempting distractions to devote ourselves to a good book. As Sara reminds us, when we read a well-written story full of truth, beauty, and goodness, we enter into a deeply satisfying conversation that affects our lives.

Where do we begin with a struggling student? In steadfast adherence to her metaphor, Sara quotes a running coach: "You have to start where you are, not where you think you should be." She refers to placement assessments that can help.

But by the end of the book, we see that Sara is no longer merely a runner in this race; she has become the coach she intended to find. In doing so, through *Reading for the Long Run*, Sara Osborne has become a faithful friend in bringing a classical Christian education to any child.

CHERYL SWOPE, M.Ed., is author of *Simply Classical: A Beautiful Education for Any Child* (Memoria Press) and creator of the Simply Classical Curriculum for children with learning challenges ages 2–21, SimplyClassical.com.

Introduction

Every maternal instinct within me cried out in protest. Still, I willed myself forward, carrying my infant child over to a stranger wearing scrubs in the pediatric surgery unit. Few moments in my life had ever called for this kind of courage, and I struggled to find fortitude for the task. Squelching the emotions which threatened to erupt, I choked back my tears and placed the small body of my firstborn son into the nurse's arms. I kissed his soft cheek and lifted a silent prayer, watching with equal parts hope and fear as he disappeared down the long white hallway. *Now we wait.*

It had been an unusually challenging morning at the hospital. Our son's scheduled eye surgery date happened to coincide with one of Kansas City's infamous tornadoes, resulting in numerous questions and long delays. We sat for hours in the waiting room, uncertain of how our long-anticipated plans might change. Hospital staffers moved bookcases and end tables out of the room, and nurses recorded the number in our family group—presumably to verify our family's survival should the situation turn disastrous. I couldn't feed my child due to surgery restrictions, yet I held him against my chest, doing my best to comfort him amidst my own swirling anxieties.

Waiting wasn't anything new to us. Of course, there had been the typical nine months of waiting for our son's arrival. But there had also been months of waiting to see if our son's eyes would align appropriately—first on their own, then aided by weeks of eye patching. We waited to discover his visual abilities. Then we waited for appointment after appointment, hoping to discover some progress from our interventions. Now, after an exhausting week of decision-making, anticipation, and interrupted schedules, we waited again for the results of his first surgery, hoping to give our son the lifelong gift of binocular sight.

When You Just Keep Waiting

Most parents realize up front that they will wait approximately forty weeks before they will meet their new baby. However, many are caught off guard by an unusually long and arduous wait for their child to arrive at certain developmental milestones. Some children walk, talk, and lose baby teeth precisely according to the pediatrician's suggested schedule; others start moving so early they seem destined for speed. Still others seem unconcerned with anyone's particular schedule for them, moving along at a developmental pace all their own. This trend continues as children move from infancy to preschool to kindergarten, developing at different intervals and speeds.

When a child is ready to enter school, however, the developmental milestones that most parents have waited for become more important and fraught with concern: *When will my child learn his alphabet? When will she tie her shoes? Why can't he write his name? Will she ever be able to keep up with her peers? Will he ever learn to read?* Kindergarten entrance exams loom ahead like the gates to an off-limits castle, and primary school reading assessments and progress reports produce frustration and fear. Parents who feel otherwise equipped to lead their children through the passage of childhood suddenly find themselves confused, unprepared, and afraid.

Perhaps this frustration and fear is nowhere more prominent than in the parents of non-reading students. Reading is the most foundational skill in education, especially in the logocentric classical Christian model. It forms the platform on which all other language skills are based, and by it children gain access to literature, history, science, and the Bible. In the initial primary grades, children learn to read, but quite soon they read to learn. Children who cannot readily do this run the risk of being excluded from the exercises and experiences that shape a distinctly classical education. In fact, they risk being excluded from the exchange of ideas implicit in the formative education of any child. Parents of struggling readers are rightly concerned; achieving the goal of reading proficiency is a worthy endeavor. However, for some students, it is also a long journey.

Going the Distance

Amidst our own family's journey of sorting through eye surgeries, vision therapy appointments, psychological testing, play therapy sessions, and meetings with educators, we came to an uncomfortable conclusion: no one had an answer for us—at least not one single solution that would solve all of our son's educational problems. Despite many helpful insights from trained professionals, there wasn't a diagnosis that would eliminate the challenges facing our son and our family. We were left to soak in the reality that the path forward was going to be a marathon, not a sprint.

Most of us aren't born marathoners. Finishing a long-distance race requires commitment, discipline, and immense effort. However, a glimpse at the finish line of any long-distance race will dispel the assumption that only seasoned, elite runners can accomplish this goal. At nearly any long-distance race, eighty-year-old men in wool socks and street shorts line up next to outfitted gear junkies, and the obligatory college student in a banana suit stands next to a thirty-something mom in a pink tutu. Regardless of the path each person has taken to arrive at the start line, *they are all runners.*

Readers, like runners, also come in a variety of shapes, sizes, and speeds. Some have been reading with lightning speed since kindergarten, devouring book after book with joy and ease. Some read slowly but meticulously, soaking up all of the details of a story. Others read only out of obligation and struggle, hoping to make it to the last page. But *they're all readers.*

Teaching any struggling student to read is a long-distance goal. It requires commitment, discipline, and immense effort. Some days are beautiful, and progress is evident; other days are so hard that you feel tempted to quit the process altogether. Yet, like training for a long-distance race, there are tools available for anyone who is willing to pursue the goal. And those tools can carry even the most unlikely readers across the finish line of reading proficiency and into the reading life.

Hope & Help for the Journey

The goal of this book is to provide you with some tested tools to help you develop a plan, stay the course, and cross the finish line with your struggling reader. Maybe you never saw yourself as a reading instructor, researcher, motivational speaker, or coach—yet you now find yourself to be a strange mixture of all four because a child you love is struggling to read. Let me assure you: you are not alone, there is real help for the journey, and the education of your child is worth the effort it will entail. This is not a message from a pocket of sideline cheerleaders; I speak as a fellow runner, breathing hard beside you on a long, rocky trail.

In this book, you will find hope and encouragement for the daunting task of helping a struggling reader achieve his or her educational goals. To ground our discussion, we'll first explore a vision of the reading life, examining such fruits as opportunity, understanding, community, beauty, and joy. We'll also establish a clear view of our task, our student(s), and ourselves—foundational components of the journey. With a refined focus and awareness of our route, we'll discuss three necessary components of good preparation: a knowledgeable coach, the right equipment, and an appropriate training schedule for the task. We'll focus on characteristics of good training, such as appropriate pace, repetition, and consistency. Then we'll spend some time considering motivation—a key factor in student success. In an effort to avoid pitfalls, we'll discuss important ways to support your reader. Then, finally, we'll envision together what your student's "finish line" might look like, gaining a better perspective of how success should be defined.

At the end of chapters 1 and 2, you'll notice some "Notes from the Trainer" by Dr. Kevin Clark, founder and president of the Ecclesial Schools Initiative and co-author of *The Liberal Arts Tradition: A Philosophy of Christian Classical Education*. In these sections, Kevin offers a perspective shaped by seventeen years of experience in classical education, spanning the roles of teacher, academic dean, and founding head. He presents a compelling vision of the reading life, motivation for pursuing such a goal with struggling students, and a view of what this can look like on the average school day.

At the end of chapters 3–7, you will find additional "Notes from the Trainer" from optometrist Dr. David Pierce. In these sections, Dr. Pierce answers a few questions related to each chapter's content, speaking from decades of experience in treating vision-related learning problems. His insights and illustrations offer another perspective on the task of training a struggling reader. As evidenced in the following pages, his passion for serving children with learning challenges has extended into our own family, helping to fuel our persistence during days of frustration and doubt.

Unlikely Beginnings

I never planned to be a reading teacher. I am a college instructor by profession, happily leaving the primary school to those more fitted for the task. But I wanted my children to have an excellent education, and at four years old, our firstborn daughter was ready to begin that endeavor. A harried search for kindergarten programs accepting four-year-olds ensued, and I found myself out of options—except one: I could teach her myself. With a hefty dose of inspiration from *The Well-Trained Mind*,[1] and the step-by-step instructions of *The Ordinary Parent's Guide to Teaching Reading*,[2] my daughter and I struck off on an adventure together that would change both of us.

This pattern repeated for my second child—another daughter— whom I taught to read according to the same method around age five. For both of my daughters, the methodical trot through daily lessons was at some point interrupted by what can only be described as an "Aha!" moment in which the building blocks of language were suddenly available for the task of reading. After experiencing this phenomenon twice, I naively assumed this was the way of it for teaching *all* children to read. One simply needed to progress through a number of lessons until one day the child "got it" and took over the reins of reading herself.

Several years later, I sat reading to another child. He squirmed and shifted, eyes darting around the room and to my face, but rarely fixed on the book in progress. He hovered close as I turned each page, but the magic was missing—he didn't love the stories. In fact, it grew difficult to lure him into the pages of any book. By age four, he had

1. Susan Wise Bauer and Jesse Wise, *The Well-Trained Mind: A Guide to Classical Education at Home* (New York: Norton, 2009).
2. Jessie Wise and Sara Buffington, *The Ordinary Parent's Guide to Teaching Reading* (Charles City: Peace Hill Press, 2005).

endured months of eye patching and two eye muscle surgeries, and by age five we were asking questions about his development compared to his peers. His frequent fits and meltdowns at home left more questions than answers, and we struggled to figure out how his behavior might correlate with his vision problems. Eye specialist visits and school entrance testing revealed few enough "red flags" that our son's academic progress wasn't impeded by his performance, but every experience we were having at home felt metaphorically stamped "different"!

After assessments and meetings and questions and research and more questions, we decided our son needed to repeat kindergarten in an effort to build up his not-yet-blossoming basic reading skills. A new teacher offered some new perspective, we began weekly vision therapy sessions at a nearby clinic, and I worked with him one-on-one to build visual processing skills four additional days a week. He made slow and steady progress, but still did not respond to books the way my daughters had. He was now seven, and only reading a handful of words on his own—inconsistently at that.

With first grade at our children's classical school came increased information, greater exposure to literature, and more difficult words to decipher. Vacillating between hope and frustration, my husband and I pressed on, determined to provide the same education for our son that our daughters were now enjoying in full bloom. We shouldered the burden as best we could: I met my son at school every morning for a half hour of vision therapy, prodded him through evening homework, and spent much of my spare time reading and researching. I read about visual processing, dyslexia, and the science of reading. I read biographies of children with special needs being educated classically. I scoured journals and websites and did my best to sift through philosophy, opinion, and strategy to find tools to help my son. I was frustrated by the mismatches of curriculum that I felt were impeding his progress, overwhelmed by the task of homework triage, and growing increasingly angry that I couldn't find my way in the dark to the "switch" that I so desperately wanted to flip on his behalf.

Running the Race

On the hardest of days, I often took to pounding out my frustrations on the pavement, one mile at a time. Running has become an old friend over the past twenty years. It's a gift that has helped me through times of frustration, stress, sadness, and pain. It has also provided space for creative thought, motivation to persevere, and hope for overcoming challenges. My running life has often provided insight and encouragement for the long-range endeavor of training our struggling reader. The further we push forward towards reading proficiency, the more I feel like we're somewhere in the middle of a long run—one that requires the same kind of discipline, commitment, and endurance as helping a struggling reader. The process of training for a long-distance race informs the pages of this book, but—like any metaphor—the comparison doesn't extend equally to every facet of learning to read. However, as is the power of metaphor, it has helped me understand something I didn't know (how to help my struggling reader) by reflecting on something I do know (how to train for a long-distance race).

Maybe you have another passion that has required an immense amount of time and tenacity. While this book has been shaped by my experience as a runner, it is not a book written only *for* runners. It is a book about developing a plan, working hard, and staying the course—skills any serious hobby requires. If you're the parent or teacher of a struggling reader, I don't have to tell you the task requires a considerable amount of time, energy, and attention. It's easy to feel overwhelmed, to lose motivation, or to burn out completely. I hope the stories in this book will remind you that you are not alone, and that your goal is a worthy one.

This book is not primarily a guide to the latest research and methodology in teaching children with special needs how to read, although it will include some of both. Instead, it's a collection of insights and reflections that are meant to encourage families experiencing a wide variety of difficulties and disabilities in the often-daunting task of guiding, teaching, and parenting a struggling reader. Research abounds on the myriad difficulties children can face when learning to read—and offers real insights into helping your child—but methodology is only one piece of the puzzle. It can't hold your hand on the most wearisome days.

The End Goal

Author, researcher, and parent Maryanne Wolf offers a glimpse into a world where struggling students don't cross the finish line of learning to read:

> With sudden and complex clarity I saw what would happen if . . . children could not learn the seemingly simple act of passage into a culture based on literacy. They would never fall down a hole and experience the exquisite joys of immersion in the reading life. They would never discover Dinotopia, Hogwarts, Middle Earth, or Pemberley. They would never wrestle through the night with ideas too large to fit within their smaller worlds. They would never experience the great shift that moves from reading about characters like the Lightning Thief and Matilda to believing they could become heroes and heroines themselves. And most important of all, they might never experience the infinite possibilities within their own thoughts that emerge whole cloth from each fresh encounter with worlds outside their own. I realized in a whiplash

burst that . . . children . . . might never reach their full potential as human beings if they never learned to read.[3]

For Christians, the full potential of humanity is bound up in a word—the Word. The great end of humanity is not to become literate; however, let us not discount the loss when literacy is not achieved. As a parent of a struggling reader, this pursuit requires more from you than from the average parent. This may not be a race you—or your child—signed up for, but crossing the finish line is worth the effort. With a clear goal in sight, a workable plan, and a little help from a trainer, your struggling learner can make steady progress towards becoming a lifelong reader. It's a race worth running.

Ready? Set. Go!

3. Maryann Wolf, *Reader Come Home: The Reading Brain in a Digital World* (New York: HarperCollins, 2018), 4–5.

The Reading Life

In moments of acute honesty, I have questioned the importance of teaching my son to read.

The modern world accommodates non-readers to some extent—audiobooks for learning and entertainment, videos to explain testing and procedures, photos and diagrams for safety warnings and explanations. I never believed my child to be less valuable as a non-reader. While I regularly toss out the word "formative" in conversations about purposeful education, I never viewed my non-reader as somehow *unformed*. The questions came to me softly at first, clothed in doubt: *Is learning to read really a necessity for a child with visual processing challenges? Why are you making this such a priority? Do you want this for him or for yourself?* Then the voice came closer and louder: *What will it cost him? What will it cost you?* Then, finally: *Is it worth it?*

I knew the answer before the whisper could leave my lips: *yes*.

Yes, teaching my child to read is worth the effort, the energy, the time, the struggle—for him and for me. Sometimes I feel this truth in the depths of my soul. Sometimes I preach it to myself through choked-back tears. But always I know it: *a reading life may be one of the greatest gifts I ever give my children.*

In moments of doubt, it makes sense to engage in honest reflection. Certainly, a healthy self-assessment and robust examination of motives for any long-term endeavor are warranted from time to time. Wisdom might even suggest consulting experienced voices and trusted friends. We are, after all, prone to selfish pursuits and often blind to our greatest weaknesses. Sometimes conversations with others help us sift through our own desires with a clarity we cannot achieve alone. In fact, it is through dialogue with those I hold in highest regard that I have found affirmation of the importance of the reading journey. Some of those conversations have occurred with trusted friends; unsurprisingly, the majority have taken place in books.

C. S. Lewis once wrote, "Those of us who have been true readers all our life seldom fully realize the enormous extension of our being which we owe to authors."[1] The fullness of my own life is a testimony to the power of the written word. From a young age, my life has been shaped by books. As a child, mysteries and mythology swept me up in good stories, gifting me with opportunities to encounter new places and people, grow my imagination, and even know myself better. As a teenager, I read for discovery, to understand something about the world I inhabited as I struggled to find my place in it. As a young adult, I read in pursuit of Truth, to shore up my convictions and examine them for honesty and viability. I read for self-examination, to understand my identity and the identity of the God who made me thus. The shifting responsibilities of adulthood have driven me to books for intellectual and spiritual growth, to enter important conversations, and for catharsis and beauty. Many books along the way have sparked joy

---

1. C. S. Lewis, *The Reading Life: The Joy of Seeing New Worlds Through Others' Eyes*, ed. David C. Downing and Michael G. Maudlin (London: William Collins, 2019), 8.

in the midst of sadness, enraptured me with their beauty, or whisked me away when I felt trapped—geographically or otherwise. A few have utterly transformed me—named longings and passions and questions and truths in such a way that I felt searched out and known by the authors themselves. Given my own history and love of reading, one might argue that I am simply seeking to impose my own experience on a child who may be altogether different than me. If that is true, I am certainly not alone. The world echoes with testimonies of the good fruit of the reading life.

An Open Door: Access to Information and Ideas

Authors Walcutt, Lamport, and McCracken write that "reading opens a thousand doors to life."[2] The same text argues that the goal of the reading life "is . . . enlarged intellectual horizons, which lead to spiritual and personal growth, to increased opportunity, and to occasions for pleasure and gratification that are otherwise inaccessible."[3] Indeed, the act of reading gives students *access* to ideas beyond their own. Most students probably see reading as a means to gaining information and knowledge—which it is—but I daresay that's not the sole meaning of "open[ing] a thousand doors to life." Such doorways do far more than point us toward information; they lead us into new ways of thinking, feeling, seeing, and imagining. Karen Swallow Prior reminds us that "to read well is not to scour books for lessons on *what* to think. Rather, to read well is to be formed in *how* to think."[4] Reading not only broad-

2. Charles Child Walcutt, Joan Lamport, and Glenn McCracken, *Teaching Reading* (New York: Macmillan, 1974), 24.
3. Ibid.
4. Karen Swallow Prior, *On Reading Well: Finding the Good Life Through Great Books* (Grand Rapids: Brazos Press, 2018), 18.

ens intellectual horizons by giving the mind access to knowledge; it enlarges our capacity for thought by helping us learn how to engage with the realm of ideas. Reading leads us into "the great conversation"[5] that has been going on for thousands of years; it opens doors to dialogue that has shaped human civilization as we know it and is shaping us still.

Any effort to enter into the rich stream of human thought, innovation, achievement, and creativity requires reading. This is the impetus for great books programs around the country: reading works that have significantly influenced our views of God, man, the state, the church, education, philosophy, science, and art gives students a foundation from which to construct their own thoughts and questions. We cannot *ask* figures in history about their ideas, experiences, failures, and successes—but we can *read* about them. We read for access to the human imagination, a world of ideas that would be lost to us save for the privilege of the written word.

Freedom & Opportunity

Such access is not free for the taking—or at least not for all people. History reveals numerous examples of illiteracy used as a weapon of oppression. The life of former slave Frederick Douglass offers a compelling story of such power. In his memoir, Douglass reflects on the liberating effect of reading:

5. Robert M. Hutchins used the term "the Great Conversation" to refer to interaction with the (written) masterpieces of the Western tradition. He writes, "It is the task of every generation to reassess the tradition in which it lives, to discard what it cannot use, and to bring into context with the distant and intermediate past the most recent contributions to the Great Conversation." See Robert M. Hutchins, *The Great Conversation: The Substance of a Liberal Education*, Great Books of the Western World 1 (Chicago: William Benton, 1952), xi.

It was a new and special revelation, explaining dark and mysterious things, with which my youthful understanding had struggled, but struggled in vain. I now understood what had been to me a most perplexing difficulty—to wit, the white man's power to enslave the black man. It was a grand achievement, and I prized it highly. From that moment, I understood the pathway from slavery to freedom . . . Though conscious of the difficulty of learning without a teacher, I set out with high hope, and a fixed purpose, at whatever cost of trouble, to learn how to read.[6]

Douglass saw the pathway from slavery to freedom as beginning through the doorway of reading. His discovery echoes in the stories of countless other enslaved individuals.[7] Such stories reflect the common theme of education as liberation, and this through learning to read—an endeavor undertaken with a keen awareness of the potential cost.

Indeed, reading provides access to opportunity for marginalized communities across the globe, regardless of race, socioeconomic status, national identity, or geographic location. The reading life does not merely open pathways to important information and ideas formerly out of reach (which are themselves important tools for free and informed interaction within society), but it serves as a catalyst for innovation and hope: "Being steeped in excellent and visionary texts awakens us to possibilities we might have never considered—and this has been especially true for the oppressed."[8] While I wouldn't label a struggling reader as "oppressed," a child who never learns to read risks

6. Frederick Douglass, *Narrative of the Life of Frederick Douglass: An American Slave* (New York: Chartwell, 2015), 42.

7. For an excellent discussion of this topic, see Angel Adams Parham and Anika Prather, *The Black Intellectual Tradition* (Camp Hill: Classical Academic Press, 2022).

8. Parham and Prather, *Black Intellectual Tradition*, 98.

similar manipulation and coercion by those in power over him. Reading is a liberating act. It produces agency, a sense of independence and freedom of thought. This access to ideas and understanding is a most precious gift—one that is worth laboring over in pursuit of liberty.

Giving Words to Thought

Reading frees the mind through understanding the messages of others, but it also gives us language by which we understand ourselves. Self-expression may be one of the choicest fruits of the reading life: finding words to utter thoughts that had formerly "died away for want of utterance."[9] Roosevelt Montás speaks of unearthing this discovery as a young immigrant reading the words of St. Augustine: "Perhaps *Confessions* was particularly compelling to me because in it I found a language for inner exploration."[10] Feeling displaced and alone, the words of a fourth-century theologian offered Montás the language he needed to engage his own struggles. Augustine's words gave voice to ideas consistent with the human condition across time and space. What would he have missed had Montás not owned the skill to read this historic text?

Inner exploration is not a speedy act. Personal reflection requires observation, focus, and the willingness to linger over a view of ourselves long enough to form a coherent critique. Reading forces us into this pace of thinking unlike any other pursuit. In short: reading *slows us down*. In this way, slower readers may actually have the advantage![11]

---

9. Douglass, *Narrative of the Life of Frederick Douglass*, 50.

10. Roosevelt Montás, *Rescuing Socrates: How the Great Books Changed My Life and Why They Matter for a New Generation* (Princeton: Princeton University Press, 2021), 9.

11. Prior, *On Reading Well*, 17.

Encountering Otherness, Discovering Self

The reading life offers us plentiful opportunities to know both ourselves and those most unlike us; it presents us with profound moments for experiencing otherness. We read books and stories that are not our own, meeting along the way characters and thoughts that both mirror and oppose us. C. S. Lewis writes that we read to "seek an enlargement of our being. . . . We want to see with other eyes, to feel with other hearts."[12] Karen Swallow Prior quotes moral philosopher Martha Nussbaum on the view-broadening power of literature: "We have never lived enough. Our experience is, without fiction, too confined and too parochial. Literature extends it, making us reflect and feel about what might otherwise be too distant for feeling."[13]

The reading life propels us headlong into an examination of *otherness*—a lens by which we see others' hopes, struggles, strengths, and failures in ways we might otherwise never experience. Somehow, by entering into the life of another, the reader gains both a capacity for empathy and an enlargement of his own self-awareness. This is the work of character transformation: "Reading literature, more than informing us, forms us."[14]

Aristotle would house this experience under the heading of "a life of contemplation." Following his lead, Maryann Wolfe argues that there is a similar facet of the reading life—a life of reflection—in which "we enter a totally invisible, personal realm, our private 'holding ground' where we can contemplate all manner of human existence and ponder a universe whose real mysteries dwarf any of our imagina-

---

12. Lewis, *The Reading Life* 3–7.
13. Prior, *On Reading Well*, 28.
14. Ibid., 22.

tion."[15] Here we ask our deepest questions, ponder our own identities, and search for meaning. The reading life guides us in this endeavor. Roosevelt Montás remembers his own formation through reading:

> That inward education came slowly, almost unconsciously. It was not like the flipping of a switch, but like the dawning of a day. Many of the conversations we had in the classroom about the books and ideas that were rushing upon us went over my head, but like a recurring tide that leaves behind a thin layer of sediment each time it comes, eventually forming recognizable structures, the intensive reading and twice-weekly discussions . . . were co-alescing into an altogether new sense of who I was and of the possibilities of my life.[16]

We were not made for isolation. Deep dives into *otherness* through reading enlarge our views of both humanity and self. We cannot remain unaffected; seeing through the eyes of others serves to clarify our own vision, and reading gives us the lenses with which to do this. Lewis writes of such experience:

> But in reading great literature I become a thousand men and yet remain myself. Like the night sky in the Greek poem, I see with a myriad eyes, but it is still I who see. Here, as in worship, in love, in moral action, and in knowing, I transcend myself; and am never more myself than when I do.[17]

---

15. Maryann Wolf, *Reader Come Home: The Reading Brain in a Digital World* (New York: HarperCollins, 2018), 190.

16. Montás, *Rescuing Socrates*, 19.

17. Lewis, *The Reading Life Eyes*, ed. David C. Downing and Michael G. Maudlin (London: William Collins, 2019), 9.

Inhabiting Story

I can't help but think that this liberating, intoxicating, identity-forming work of the reading life owes its success—at least in part—to *story*. The powerful vehicle of story sweeps us into a plot and gives us the eyes to experience joy or sorrow through another character. By this, we sense both the significance of each individual tale as well as the grandeur of the greater story we all inhabit as joint members of humanity. Story shapes us in profound ways.

In his highly instructive book *How to Read Slowly*, James W. Sire articulates the profound power of story:

> In great literature—poetry and fiction—we see ourselves, our friends, our enemies, the world around us. We see our interests portrayed in bold relief—our questions asked better than we can ask them, our problems pictured better than we can picture them by ourselves, our fantasies realized beyond our fondest dreams, our fears confirmed in horrors more horrible than our nightmares, our hopes fulfilled past our ability to yearn or desire. . . . Life, our life is short, but art is long. Sophocles is dead, but Oedipus lives on and on, and is recreated hundreds of thousands of times as generation after generation brings him to life by reading *Oedipus Rex* or seeing it performed on stage. Each of us when we read a great piece of literature is a little more human than before, a little more able to say with meaning, "This, then, is man."[18]

I still remember reading Jean Craighead George's *My Side of the Mountain* and Gary Paulsen's *Hatchet* when I was nine years old. In those

18. James W. Sire, *How to Read Slowly: Reading for Comprehension* (Colorado Springs: Waterbrook Press, 1989), 58–59.

pages, I was Sam Gribley; I became Brian. My childhood mind didn't seem to care that both characters were boys! I still saw through their eyes and inhabited their stories. Something within me resonated with their keen awareness of nature, their independence, their instincts for survival—and also their loneliness. I relished their individual adventures, but I sensed in both characters a longing for community, belonging, and love. Their stories weren't meant to exist in isolation; they declared something true of all humanity: we inhabit a story larger than our own.

As a child, imagining others' stories gave me a fuller understanding of myself as well as a sense of the human journey. As an adult, I still experience this gift. I seek it, too, for my children: I want to offer them story upon story to step into and draw from as they orient themselves to the family of humanity. Can this be done without a reading life?

A Shared Community

Gaining a fuller understanding of community is not a task relegated to young or adolescent readers. Adult readers need the same reminders that we are not alone; someone else across time or space is inhabiting the same kind of story. Sometimes we come to this truth through fiction; however, I recently encountered it through the beginning pages of *The Black Intellectual Tradition* by Drs. Angel Adams Parham and Anika Prather. In her introductory comments, Parham reveals a trajectory not unlike my own: we were both mothers of preschoolers who hinted at a need for an education beyond what we knew how to give; we had both been shaped by literature and strived to steep our homes in the richness of good books; we both learned alongside our children, sometimes reading the classics for the first time ourselves; we both struggled to juggle a teaching and intellectual life alongside homeschooling; we both looked for ways to supplement a child's education outside of what a school could offer him; we both have husbands who championed all these pursuits and in no small way made our classical educational journeys possible. Within a few pages, I felt I had both met a new friend and seen a reflection of myself. Despite our different cultural and geographic backgrounds, and the fact that we have never met, the knowledge that someone else had pursued such a similar path reminded me anew that I am not alone. Reading further into *The Black Intellectual Tradition* only offers further reminders of the shared human spirit that unifies the most diverse backgrounds. In so many ways, "we read to know that we are not alone"[19]—a transformational consolation.

Beauty & Pleasure

We are transformed by far more than connection, exploration, otherness, or knowledge; the sheer beauty of written words yields a kind of pleasure that adds to the richness of the human experience. Written words themselves wield a strange kind of power, harnessing all manner of thought in just a few blackened letters. The best wordsmiths take these lumps of clay and form them into sentences that heighten our senses, captivate us with wonder, and please us with shape, rhythm, and rhyme. Not unlike a potter building a pot with coils, those sentences lay atop one another to create a vessel of beauty and function, a work of art that holds messages and ideas birthed in the imagination of another. Poetry, fiction, memoir, non-fiction prose—here words *sing*, affecting us deeply, as if taking in the sound of a master orchestra, each instrument playing its own notes in melody and harmony. Here, reading enfolds us with beauty and leads us to pleasure.

Such beauty is profoundly comforting. I was recently reminded of this by my youngest child, who had been battling bad dreams during

---

19. The actor playing C. S. Lewis utters this statement in the film *Shadowlands*.

his nighttime sleep. After I tucked in his blankets, said a prayer, and sang his evening lullaby, he offered up an unusual request for an eight-year-old boy: he asked me to read "A Liturgy for One Who Has Suffered a Nightmare" from Douglas McKelvey's *Every Moment Holy*.[20] Not one to turn down a chance to read poetic prayers to my children, I quickly obliged, and my once-wary child drifted off to sleep. The liturgy's soothing effects were not solely due to its content—my own prayer had verbalized the same truths; additional consolation came from its beauty. My child slept the whole night through.

Sometimes the beauty and pleasure of written words come to us on a grander scale—in the exquisite arc of a storyline or the utter genius of its ending. We witness it when a character is so wonderfully created that we feel he could be our neighbor next door—we can almost smell his clothes, feel his breath, touch the curl of his hair. We encounter it when a fiction story carries us into worlds so unlike our own that we nearly burst with the joy of exploration and imagination, sensing that we ourselves were created to be co-creators, finding pleasure in the art of making something yet unknown.

We belong to a broken world of pain, ailments, and limitations, yet reading reminds us that beauty still abounds—sometimes in our world, sometimes just beyond it—and pleasure overflows at the pages of well-written texts. Beauty isn't an add-on to the human experience, a frivolity that we can do without; it enriches us, fills us, and in many ways sustains us in a journey that promises suffering and sorrow. I want my children to have every access to this grace along their own rock-strewn paths.

20. Douglas Kaine McKelvey, *Every Moment Holy* (Nashville: Rabbit Room Press, 2017), 193–94.

Cultivating Character

Reading is a remarkable resource for an education that pursues beauty; it is likewise a conduit for the cultivation of character. Author and theologian Vigen Guroian argues that stories furnish a virtuous education in a way that other forms of instruction cannot:

> Mere instruction in morality is not sufficient to nurture the virtues. It might even backfire, especially when the presentation is heavily exhortative and the pupil's will is coerced. Instead, a compelling vision of the goodness of goodness itself needs to be presented in a way that is attractive and stirs the imagination. A good moral education addresses both the cognitive and affective dimensions of human nature. Stories are an irreplaceable medium for this kind of moral education—that is, the education of character.[21]

By offering a powerful mirror of the human experience, stories have the capacity to shape who we become. We see the consequence of choices, good and bad, and grow in an awareness of how complex those categories can be: characters who seem good make bad choices, and one-time scoundrels experience redemption and restoration. We begin to sense good and evil, friend and foe, fear and courage—and perhaps find the desire to *be* a good and courageous friend. Through considering the choices of others, we begin to make our own. Owning the skills of language decoding and comprehension does not equate to possessing virtuous character; however, non-readers do lack something of significance as they wrestle to make sense of the human experience.

---

21. Vigen Guroian, *Tending the Heart of Virtue: How Classic Stories Awaken a Child's Moral Imagination* (New York: Oxford University Press, 1998), 20.

The ability to read independently gives a person a ready entrance into exploring the good life and gaining its fruits. It's a doorway I want to hold open for my child—and for all struggling readers.

CH. 1 "NOTES FROM THE TRAINER": A FEW QUESTIONS & ANSWERS FROM DR. KEVIN CLARK

How does the reading life not just teach a student what *to think, but* how *to think?*

Because reading requires the habit of imagination—to borrow Charlotte Mason's idea—because it's an active process, we have to exercise the effort of looking along the horizon alongside the author, and that's a work of creative imagination. It isn't that people either have imagination or don't—it's something trained in us. Imagination is a skill that is taught early in grammar school in the classical model. Students learn how to enter into a text, to follow a line of thought that an author is developing.

The more you read, the more you hone the ability to see the world the way the author is describing it. That takes practice. The reading life promotes that ability. It also enables you to do that with real people, not just texts: I'm able to follow someone's point as he or she develops it. In that moment, I experience the exciting point of both having my expectations met and being surprised—the message is neither too familiar nor too strange. The reading life enables us to have that experience in real life because we've developed the habits of attention and imagination through interacting with a text.

Some of our students have a unique configuration of challenges that make reading difficult: dyslexia, dysgraphia, and ADHD. Yet we require all our students to build up the habit of reading each night. For some of them it's a real struggle, and I have parents who ask, "Is it okay to listen to a recording and try to follow along?" My answer is, "Yes, absolutely!" Learning to listen to a text is a part of reading. Learning to follow a text's line of thinking is a part of learning to read well. It's a task which requires an active imagination—and by listening and following along, students necessarily build up the habits of attention and endurance and stamina.

How is the reading life a liberating one?

A great inheritance of ideas and ideals sits before us as an open secret, but it remains a secret if you don't know how to read. I think of C. S. Lewis's words in "Learning in War-Time" when he talks about how the scholar has lived at all times in all places because he has entered into that experience through reading.[22] If we don't have the ability to read, our experience of life will be small and truncated—bound to our own experience, our own time, our own perspective. Reading is a way that I expand my capacity to understand more and experience more. It affects the way I live and interact with others, my expectations of what there is to know and what there is to learn.

Reading also enables us to be at home in language. Think of this inheritance of ideas and ideals as a place: you don't feel at home in that place if you can't read. You always feel like a stranger; you're on the outside. Through reading, we are literally "rehabilitating" our students—we are bringing them *home* through reading.

22. C. S. Lewis, "Learning in War-Time." Transcript of speech delivered at the Church of St. Mary the Virgin, Oxford, 1939. www.christendom.edu/wp-content /uploads/2021/02/Learning-In-Wartime-C.S.-Lewis-1939.pdf.

How does the reading life contribute to moral formation and character development?

If I'm going to read you, I have to listen to what you say. The only way I can understand you is if I think you have something to tell me and if you're understandable. So the very beginning of my encounter with you as a text is to treat you like a person, to be patient, to have my mouth closed and my ears open, to show you respect. Even if I'm going to disagree with you, I have to understand you first.

The posture necessary for reading is receptive, and it is patient. There is a baseline of humility. These are key points of moral formation and character development that we desire in classical Christian education. Reading is an academic practice that creates a certain habit of heart and mind that is essential for the moral life, the godly life.

It's like an analogy of grace: you have to receive the word through reading. It's receptive. The goods that come from reading have to be received. I come to them with my hands open, desiring them, but I have to receive them from outside myself. Learning to do this creates a posture towards what is *real* and the expectation that good things are received over time. Patience, perseverance—they're both bound up in reading.

Aristotle argued that young people are poor hearers of lectures on ethics because they lack experience in the affairs of life. You can only get experience in the affairs of life by living life—or by reading texts, where you gain access to other lived experience through the imagination! In this way, even people with young heads on their shoulders are able to have experienced minds. We don't only lean on personal experience to provide the imaginative framework necessary for understanding our reality on any given day; reading also creates this.

Know Your Route:
Understanding the Task Before You

My running life has gifted me with joys not entirely unlike those of the reading life. Long runs down quiet roads have offered hours for contemplation and self-reflection, the rhythm of my footfall sounding off like a drumbeat to a melody of wandering thoughts. Like reading, long runs require a pace that slows me down from the sprint of daily tasks; I am left with only myself to examine and interact with, mile after mile. Pursuing new distances compounds this phenomenon as I wrestle with self-doubt and dreams, limitations and achievement. Distance running requires something of me, and I find that after a period of initial hesitation, I give it willingly: I submit myself to a training process that will leave me transformed. By it, I will gain new-found physical strength and mental tenacity, but I will also develop an attitude of perseverance—a byproduct of learning that I can, in fact, do difficult things.

Perhaps more than anything, my running life has demonstrated to me the end product of a series of choices: I didn't start my running life with any noticeable skill or natural advantage, but saying "yes" again and again to every hard hill, to each exhausting lap I didn't feel like jogging, to every long trail run in the rain, and to each additional mile of weekly distance has made me who I am as a runner. Any strength or stamina I possess is owing to the choice to run, time and time again.

As the long-distance running life appears to a novice athlete, so does the reading life to the fledgling reader—yet the simple truth still applies: he can, in fact, accomplish this difficult task. My son's reading training, like my running training, has consisted of a series of choices. He must choose again, each new day, to say *yes* to the struggle. He must say *yes* to daily lessons when his eyes are fatigued, when homework is overwhelming, when his learning environment is inhospitable. He must say *yes* when he has a cold, when he has stayed up too late, when he is tired of trying, when he feels like he is the only one traversing a rocky path. At every crisis of belief causing doubt that this endeavor is worthwhile, by the grace of God, he has chosen to say "yes"—and this series of choices has shaped us both.

The Valley of Struggle

The path to the reading life for a struggling reader is necessarily one of wrestling. He must initially wrestle with inability or difference, but no less must he grapple with emotion and will. She must fight the urge to give into despair, to refuse the lies often whispered in her quietest moments, to throw off limitations put on her by myopic bystanders. Her mind and body grow weary, and still she must attend to lessons. He needs countless more repetitions for mastery and wrestles with his need for time. She finds hope from believing she is valued by God, but she may often wonder why His love is manifest this way. In the years I've been teaching my son to read, we've visited many of these topics—conversations you might imagine too weighty or far off for a young child to handle. But wrestling with weakness is a common struggle that does not distinguish between ages.

In John 9, Jesus's disciples ask why a man was born blind at birth, seeking to correlate a particular sin with his disability. The implication of their question is that surely such a condition represents some kind of punishment—divine judgment aimed at highlighting this man's or his parents' sin and resulting in a lifetime of struggle. Jesus's response to this inquiry challenges our perceptions of disability: "Jesus answered, 'It was not that this man sinned, or his parents, but that the works of God might be displayed in him.'"[1] Somehow, in God's divine wisdom, He intended this man's disability to display the works of God. *But how?*

Serving students with disabilities is often disorienting for parents and teachers who have never been forced to approach the world through such a lens. However, students with disabilities are merely encountering a degree of weakness that will one day find us all. Author and theologian Benjamin Conner writes,

> In truth, the concept of disability is difficult to define, but one thing is certain: disability is an unsurprising aspect of being human. It is not a deficiency or the consequence of sin, and people with disabilities are to be neither pitied nor valorized because of their disability. Disability, while representing real challenges and impairments, is also a fluid category, a label, a social construction that helps people make sense of the world.[2]

The student with a disability, disorder, or difference that makes the path to learning difficult is not part of a separate community with

1. John 9:3 (ESV).

2. Benjamin T. Conner, "Ways We Worship: Disability and Worship," *Faithful Lives* 5 (2020): 83, accessed February 2, 2023, http://images.cofo.edu/cofo/about/FaithfulWorship.pdf. For a fuller discussion of theology and disability, see Benjamin T. Conner's book *Disabling Mission, Enabling Witness: Exploring Missiology Through the Lens of Disablity Studies* (Downer's Grove: IVP Academic, 2018).

separate ends; he is not ontologically *other*. Her weakness may arrive at a different time or extend to a different realm or degree than our own, but it is a common human phenomenon. In fact, weakness is a part of what it means to be human. We are not self-sufficient—struggling students know this well. What they may know less is that God's design for *all* people is for us to be sanctified and shaped by struggle. As author and theologian J. I. Packer writes, "Weakness is the way" for the Christian.[3] *The way to what?* we might well ask. *The way to true strength.* While it may sound counterintuitive to us, this is the upside-down kingdom of God at work in the world: "[God's] power is made perfect in weakness."[4] The task for parents and teachers of students with special needs is to help them make sense of this weakness as a universal aspect of being human. We must cultivate a posture of both humility and hope: "Therefore I will boast all the more gladly of my weakness, so that the power of Christ may rest upon me. For the sake of Christ, then, I am content with weaknesses. . . . For when I am weak, then I am strong."[5]

Leading a child with a disability through the way of weakness is a strange kind of gift. None of us would naturally choose struggle over ease for our child, but the difficult path to the reading life produces a kind of character that is borne through hardship. Both student and teacher are shaped by weakness—his manifest through the struggle to read, and mine through the struggle to teach him. We both bring our varied weaknesses to the task and, perhaps not unlike another young boy long ago, offer them to Jesus to bless.[6] I have little doubt

3. For a wonderful exploration of this concept in Scripture, see J. I. Packer's book *Weakness Is the Way: Life with Christ Our Strength* (Wheaton: Crossway, 2013).

4. 2 Corinthians 12:9a, (ESV).

5. 2 Corinthians 12:9b-10, (ESV).

6. John 6:9, (ESV).

that the Lord is using this challenge in both of our lives to conform us into the image of Christ. We pursue the transformative effects of this co-labor in faith: "Count it all joy, my brother, when you meet trials of various kinds, for you know that the testing of your faith produces steadfastness. And let steadfastness have its full effect, that you may be perfect and complete, lacking in nothing."[7]

Reading in the Classical School & Homeschool

Classical education emphasizes the formative power of learning through struggle: the fundamental purpose of education is to grow our children in wisdom and virtue. Wrestling with ideas and ourselves yields true transformation. While that process necessarily involves instruction and assessment, skill production is not the ultimate goal. Instead, we seek to facilitate a life of human flourishing. More than simply seeking knowledge, we pursue understanding and discernment; we applaud intellectual progress, but we treasure noble character. We wrestle with texts, ideas, and our inner man in pursuit of truth, beauty, and goodness—virtues foundational for *eudaimonia* ("the good life").

A classical view of learning believes a reading life to be a pathway to wisdom and virtue, yet this lofty goal can sometimes discourage parents of students with special needs. Parents—and sometimes teachers—wonder: *Can a child with a special learning need traverse this path? If she has a disability, can she be educated classically? Will slow processing impede his flourishing? Will she ever be able to access the ideas of the Great Conversation?* While the details of classically educating a student with special needs may be complex, the overall assessment is

7. James 1:2–4, (ESV).

truly quite simple: classical education offers an excellent education for any student.[8] In fact, such an education may offer particular benefits for struggling readers.

Meaning, Order, & Method

A classical approach to teaching reading is phonics-based; that is, students are taught letter recognition and sounds, phonograms, and word families as first steps in the reading process. They anticipate patterns and learn rules for dividing syllables. Language is broken down in an orderly fashion, even at the word level. While such a process provides an appropriate path to reading for all students, this simple, methodical approach to decoding is exactly what struggling readers need. Such students may require more time (to accommodate slower processing), more repetition (to solidify concepts and create new pathways for finding them), or altered curricula (color-coded, larger print, or fewer words on a page), but the benefits of the model are clear. In fact, author and classical educator Cheryl Lowe points out that "Orton-Gillingham phonics, which is designed for students with dyslexia, is in every respect a classic traditional phonics program."[9]

In the classical model, students with even the most basic decoding ability apply their newfound knowledge to decipher short sentences, followed by short stories or passages. Encountering real texts offers a boost of confidence and a glimpse into the reading life, a compelling taste of the fruits we diligently pursue. Every practice session offers an opportunity for teachers to help build skill and shape student desire.

8. For a winsome discussion of this argument, see Cheryl Swope's *Simply Classical: A Beautiful Education for Any Child*, 2nd ed, (Louisville: Memoria Press, 2019).

9. Cheryl Lowe, "How to Teach Phonics (Part II)," Memoria Press, accessed February 1, 2023, https://www.memoriapress.com/articles/teach-phonics-part-ii/.

Over time, students gain an awareness of the more subtle nuances of the English language—words that sound the same but have different meanings or words spelled the same but pronounced with different syllable stress. They add increasing comprehension to their decoding skills, learning to differentiate between main ideas and details as they approach increasingly difficult texts. They hear rhythm and notice rhyme. Their attention is led toward meaning and beauty—both in the substance of stories, plays, and poems and in the language itself.

With more complex texts come complicated ideas—and here the slow reader may possess a surprising asset. Such reading requires sustained attention, discipline, and numerous rounds of consideration in an effort at analysis and reflection,[10] skills that most struggling readers will develop by necessity. Through such reading—whether of a historical document, an ancient story, or a contemporary poem—students grow in their understanding of language, meaning, identity, and membership in the community of humanity. These deeper aspects of growth—the choicest fruits of the reading life—are what I desire for my struggling reader.

Ultimately, a distinctly classical education offers something to students with disabilities or significant differences that a modern approach to education simply does not: a view of learning concerned with a person, not a product. Students with special needs are often viewed as "deficient"; a component of the academic machine is missing, and it is the goal of educators and caretakers to plug the hole and get the machine up and running. A child's limited abilities are simply an interruption to progress, an irritating problem to be solved—the sooner, the better. This view stems from an altogether shaky philosoph-

---

10. For an excellent discussion of this topic, see James W. Sire's book *How to Read Slowly: Reading for Comprehension* (Colorado Springs: Waterbrook Press, 1989).

ical system that sees education as an assembly line of skill production, seeking to quickly yield a product that can function according to its programming. Reading (in truth, all learning!) becomes just another task—a skill to check off a list (for a grade, graduation, or employ-ment)—not a means to a particular kind of *living*.

To teach a struggling student—or any child—in this fashion is stifling and short-sighted. While some may deem the difficult work of a classical education to be less "efficient" for children with special needs, this long road to learning produces a kind of character, atten-tion, and even skill that is difficult to attain otherwise. Such a child will experience growth in his mind and spirit that does not end with reading proficiency. She will find that weakness is, indeed, the way to true strength; struggle, in a strange way, completes her character.[11]

Classical education regularly reminds us that raising and educating human beings is never *efficient*. We do not teach with the goal of maxi-mizing output with minimal effort; our students are not commodities to be harvested and distributed according to the world's assessed value. Our task is the cultivation of a child who bears the mark of the divine. She is something so much more than a problem to be solved—but the world of modern education will test this belief. Let me encourage you to take time to reflect on the route you've chosen to take with your struggling student. There are those who will tell you your child cannot pursue such a path—the way is too hard and the learning curve too steep—but there are so many testimonies of the opposite truth. With patient, loving labor, you can lead your child into the reading life.

11. 2 Corinthians 12:9, James 1:4, (ESV).

The Task Before You

Not every parent or teacher comes to a pursuit of the reading life with such a robust, theological, or philosophical view of its benefits—nor do we always consider the assumptions of value or inadequacy we may be harboring about our students. Perhaps deep down, you still view the task of teaching your struggling reader as a fight to make him just like his peers. Perhaps you yourself haven't tasted the fruits of the reading life that you offer to your student. Maybe you've wrestled with your struggling reader's weakness—and your own, as teacher—and wondered if the journey is worth the effort it will entail. Perhaps your student has simply tried and failed so many times that you've run out of reasons to keep prodding his progress. Maybe you feel like your paradigm for learning has come unraveled, and you can't clearly distinguish the possible from the impossible—or hope from futility.

Leading struggling students into the reading life necessitates our own wrestling with some of these questions. We need a clear view of what we're after—this kind of life that offers an open door to wonder, wisdom, and growth. We need a clear view of our students—children beset with weakness, yes, but no less children with dignity, value, aptitude, and a unique opportunity to display the works of God. We also need a clear view of ourselves—parents and teachers not entirely unlike our students, those who come to the learning task with our own set of weaknesses and inadequacies. In short, we need to *know our route*. For many of these students, we are the heralds of truth, the reminders of value, the cheerleaders of effort who have the unspeakable privilege of modeling perseverance and hope to close-watching eyes. We need a vision of success that will sustain us in the midst of this labor.

DO YOU KNOW YOUR ROUTE?

1. Do you have a clear view of what you're after? What is your end goal for teaching reading? Will it sustain you in the midst of the long run to the reading life?

2. Do you have a clear view of your student? Have you made any assumptions about his/her inadequacies or value that need to be corrected?

3. Do you have a clear view of yourself, as teacher? How can you empathize with your student's weaknesses—and by doing so, model the character of Christ?[12]

12. See Hebrews 4:15, (ESV).

If your view of reading is entirely utilitarian—aimed solely at skill production for graduation or employment—as soon as an easier option presents itself, you will take it. You will exchange the difficulty of reading for the pragmatism of video learning, audio tools, and a dependence on others. But if you catch the vision of reading as a transformational experience, an individual entrance into conversation, community, beauty, imagination, and pleasure—your doubts about its value will die a thousand deaths. You will understand the value of giving all students access to this treasure. You will recognize the task of teaching reading as an opportunity to cultivate wisdom and virtue, and with that recognition find a fresh reminder for why yours is such a worthy occupation. The distance of the race may be daunting, and your own insufficiency may be staring you down, but with your eyes on the goal, you will be ready for the challenge. You will lead your student into the reading life.

Ch. 2 "Notes from the Trainer": A Few Questions & Answers from Dr. Kevin Clark

How is weakness a part of what it means to be human?

In Alasdair MacIntyre's book *Dependent Rational Animals*, he says that in the entire history of moral inquiry in the West, the assumption is that the human being in his natural state is rational and independent.[13] Yet when you look at the actual lived human life, it begins in utter dependence, it often ends in utter dependence, and it is punctuated throughout by brokenness, illness, and

---

13. Alasdair C. MacIntyre, *Dependent Rational Animals: Why Human Beings Need the Virtues* (Chicago: Open Court Publishing, 2001).

loss. Human life is not even conceivable as being human outside of a community of people who are mutually benefitting and helping one another. It's interesting, then, that we'd philosophize about human life as if we're independent when the truth of human life is dependence in every direction.

So, how is weakness a part of being human? It might just be the defining feature! It's not good for man to be alone—God created man in his upright, creational state, and there was something *not good*. He wasn't made to be independent. God's plan was always a family and always to make new humans through infancy. Weakness is bound up in the very nature of humanity.

In the Bible, St. Paul glories in his weakness. We see this in many of his letters. When he is weak, therefore—in the grace of Christ—he is strong. Again, notice the receptive aspect! We see this in the Beatitudes as well: blessed are the mournful. *Why?* Because in being mournful, you get to be comforted! Blessed are those who hunger. *Why?* Because they get to be filled with good things! In God's mysterious plan, he made humanity a fragile, embodied thing that gets to be cared for through friendship. He made us part of a family that needs to be comforted and built up. If you view weakness as an aberration of humanity, you are missing it. The entire picture shows us the opposite: weakness is actually a clue to who you are and what you're made for.

Is classical education truly an excellent education for all kinds of students?

If by a classical education you mean a liberal arts education, absolutely! Liberal arts are the skills of self-learning. If anyone is going to reach maturity, they need to hone the ability to learn for themselves, to know truth themselves—to have the confidence that comes from knowing not just what's immediately given to you, but to know how to find out truth and seek it yourself. It's the education that makes you at home in your inheritance—and who doesn't deserve that inheritance? Which students? Is it only for "Type A," high performing students? No, the opportunity to receive what's good and true and lovely is for everyone.

Of course, God has made us all different. Not everyone will absorb this type of education at the same saturation level—but everyone should have the ability to partake and to enjoy the fruits of learning. There will be different depths to which people master the arts of grammar or logic or rhetoric, but if those skills are truly liberating—if they set you free with respect to language so that you're not at the mercy of language but can use it wisely and well for loving your neighbor and loving the truth—then everyone needs that kind of learning.

I'm reminded of St. Augustine's *Confessions* where we learn that his own spiritual transformation hinged on the stories he heard of other people's conversion.[14] If, in some way, the stories that I read provide the pattern for my own life, who doesn't need the pattern? Who doesn't need the metaphors for the moral life? Who doesn't need the struggle that will produce the wrestling and perseverance toward the good life? I think everybody needs that. As a Christian, I don't know how to truly educate a child without an orientation towards truth, goodness, and beauty.

How do you support struggling readers in your classrooms?

First, we acknowledge that the struggling reader is not an anomaly and that these are children we want to serve. Interestingly, a significant insight of the Orton-Gillingham model is that the path to meeting the needs of struggling readers is actually good

14. Augustine, *The Confessions of Saint Augustine*, trans. Henry Chadwick (Oxford: Oxford University Press, 2008), 133-54.

for every single person who needs to read. For the students who encounter significant obstacles to reading—especially dyslexia—such a model helps in remarkable ways. It brings something that was once impossible suddenly within reach. For other students, it might make something that is a challenge more fruitful. Either way, teaching this way is beneficial. Reorienting your thinking about good pedagogy is critical. The way that we teach things classically is actually—at the heart—good for all students.

We also partner with specialists who help students with significant challenges, such as dyslexia, dysgraphia, dyscalculia, or other special learning needs. They get the support they need, and the specialists help us understand what it's like for these kids—for example, how they really see—which helps us appreciate the child's difficulty and remember the importance of patience. We also try to not overload students with unnecessary elements of assessment; for example, we might offer comprehension assessment orally instead of having students write a response to a prompt.

If learning language arts is about acquiring the skills of language, and my student is a struggling reader, it makes sense to use the class time devoted to reading to address that lacking skill. The student isn't going to make progress without help. Taking him out of art or gym class or nature study, which unfortunately happens in so many schools, isn't helpful. We find the area in which the child is struggling and provide the extra support they need during that time. Contrary to the way many schools address struggling learners, we have an assistant teacher stay with the "high flying" students and put the master teacher with the struggling students. That focused teaching helps them make real gains toward the reading life.

Getting Ready: Developing a Plan That Works

I was twenty years old when I started running regularly, and my first race goal—laughable though it may have been—was to run a marathon. Never having run more than a few miles at one time in my life, I was an unlikely candidate for such a feat; nevertheless, I was lured in by a goal I could plan for and seek to accomplish with some measure of control. My first months of marathon training included hours of research, planning, running, and recovering. I read books and magazines in an effort to train well. I chatted on the phone with experts and found others in my community who were interested in running. I charted distances, tracked nutrition, and swapped my shoes out at the appropriate mile-markers. With every diagonal line drawn across a calendar square in my training schedule, I inched closer toward the finish line.

All of my progress as a runner began with two essential elements: (1) an honest evaluation of my ability at the starting line, and (2) a good, workable plan. Evaluating readiness is the first step toward growth in virtually any skill, running included. I needed a plan for myself that began *where I was ready to begin*. Starting out with distances that were too long or at a speed that was too fast would have only delayed my growth as a runner (and dashed my spirits in the process). I needed a solid plan that made sense in light of my starting condition, one that allowed me to start small, build confidence, and set attainable goals. This plan needed to take a variety of factors into consideration in order to be successful—a knowledgeable coach, necessary equipment, and a workable schedule, to name a few. I needed at least one person to provide insight and prod me along on the hard days, the right shoes for my particular body mechanics, and a schedule that matched my fitness and lifestyle.

Evaluating Your Starting Point

Training a struggling learner to read requires the same approach. First, parents (with the aid of teachers, doctors, counselors, and other helpers) need to engage in an honest evaluation of their child's starting condition. Has the child failed to reach certain developmental milestones?[1] Are behavior issues interrupting academic and social progress? Are there evident mismatches in academic skills? Is she struggling to remember a lesson after it has been learned or make forward progress in a curriculum? Does he show visible signs of frustration or emotional distress? An accurate evaluation may necessitate consultations with a pediatrician, vision specialist, psychologist, school counselor, or other professional in order to identify a disability, disorder, or difference interfering with a student's reading progress. If a child is already enrolled in school, teachers and reading assessments

---

1. The American Academy of Pediatrics (AAP) and Center for Disease Control (CDC) offer a free, downloadable guide to developmental milestones at https://www.cdc.gov/ncbddd/actearly/pdf/parents_pdfs/ milestonemomentseng508.pdf. While every child's growth pattern is unique, this document offers insight into typical progress.

can offer insight into a student's specific strengths and weaknesses. If a parent is homeschooling, he or she can utilize readiness assessments offered by curriculum creators.[2] I refer to this group of people as a "team of knowers." Each person on this team knows your child in a different context. A doctor offers a medical perspective; a teacher offers an academic perspective (and sometimes a social one, as he or she watches your child interact with others); a counselor or psychologist offers a mental and emotional perspective. The combination of this knowledge offers far greater insight into the mind of your child than one perspective alone!

Another way parents can strive to reach an accurate evaluation of their child's struggles is to keep a journal, noting down specific challenges, habits, attitudes, or changes in behavior. You see and know your child more than anyone else. Keeping a record of events and experiences you observe at home often leads to the realization of patterns that characterize a child's learning experience. You may notice specific exercises, times of day, or amounts of focus that push your child to his or her limit. Consider these as clues in your investigation. All of these resources will help to inform an honest evaluation of your child's starting condition. Once you have a good idea of your child's ability, the next step is to develop a good, workable plan.

---

2. For example, Simply Classical and All About Reading both offer free online tools to evaluate a student's current academic ability and/or reading skill.

AN HONEST EVALUATION:
QUESTIONS FOR REFLECTION

1. What experiences and observations have caused concern about my student's ability to read or learn? Have others articulated similar concerns?

2. Have I gathered evidence by . . .
    - Considering how my child's progress aligns with typical developmental milestones?
    - Consulting academic assessments, reading readiness tools, or intelligence testing?
    - Checking vision and hearing ability through appropriate screenings (including tests for dyslexia and/or visual processing challenges)?
    - Obtaining a psychological evaluation of concerning behavior patterns and/or emotional health?
    - Noting my child's visible or articulated frustration at certain learning tasks?

3. Have I noticed . . .
    - Certain times of day when my student shuts down?
    - Specific skills or exercises that induce frustration?
    - Trouble focusing for extended periods of time (as evidenced by physical sensations such as eye burning/stinging -OR- by emotional outbursts/ attitude changes)?
    - Inattentiveness or refusal to engage in reading tasks?

Finding a Coach

It was an inspiring coach who prompted my start in long-distance running. My uncle served as a volunteer coach with Team in Training, helping others train for and complete long-distance races in order to raise money for charity. He was happy, dedicated, and passionate about his running. And—perhaps most importantly—he thought I could run, too. He was willing to look at a complete novice as a would-be runner, both for the sake of my own joy and achievement and for the greater cause of charity. His passion was contagious and, without a doubt, helped carry me across the first of many finish lines.

Finding a coach with knowledge and experience who also shares a passion for your child to cross the finish line of reading is an invaluable asset. Few of us begin with enough knowledge or motivation to sustain us on the most difficult days of reading training. We need help from someone who has walked the road before us. We need a coach who has an eye on both the starting line and the finish line—and a plan to get us from one to the other.

My husband and I limped through the first years of parenting a struggling learner without a relationship with any real "coaches" or "trainers." We had visited numerous doctors and specialists with our child, but we often left with more questions than answers, rarely feeling like anyone was looking at the whole picture of our child's challenges. We addressed problems only as they appeared, like a living game of "whack-a-mole," never developing a long-term plan. The familiar twin feelings of loneliness and frustration set in, and we often wondered if we'd ever find an outside voice to speak into our situation with direction and encouragement.

When a teacher in our son's school recommended visiting a nearby doctor who dealt with vision-related learning issues, we were cautiously optimistic. I scoured the clinic's website during the months leading up to our initial consultation, hoping to head off any unrealistic expectations. I researched the possibilities of unfamiliar terms. I reviewed credentials, patient testimonies, and offered services. I was tired of being disappointed.

I liked Dr. Pierce right away, and for one main reason: he clearly thought our son was amazing. I don't think I realized until that consultation how accustomed to lukewarm reception we had become. This office visit was unlike any we had previously experienced. Dr. Pierce spent nearly two hours with us, conducting a thorough vision examination, patiently asking and answering questions, often nodding in agreement with our concerns. While our son's eyes were the main focus, we discussed all kinds of difficulties we were having with his learning and behavior, striving to make sense of the overall picture of our struggling learner. When most of my questions had been answered and I started to feel like we were surely taking up half of Dr. Pierce's day, we left the office, equipped with a plan. Tears streamed down my face as I drove the hour-long commute home. I felt like someone had finally—truly, and fully—heard our concerns for our son and somehow seemed to care almost as deeply as we did. We had arrived at the vision clinic that day to see a doctor, but we left with a "coach" and a friend. His wisdom and direction have been invaluable to us over the years as we've continued to problem-solve for our son.

While having a living, breathing "coach" offers obvious benefits, we've also found wisdom, encouragement, and inspiration from guides we don't know personally. In her book *Rethinking School*,[3] Susan Wise Bauer offered us tools for educational analysis and po-

---

3. Susan Wise Bauer, *Rethinking School: How to Take Charge of Your Child's Education* (New York: W. W. Norton & Company, 2018).

tential strategies for accommodation. We also found her "thought experiments" to be both therapeutic and liberating, prompting us to think creatively and imagine the best possible education for our child. While we've never met one another, Bauer feels like an old, familiar friend cheering us along in the pursuit of an excellent education for all of our children.

Author and speaker Cheryl Swope's memoir, *Simply Classical*,[4] affected us similarly. I found in its pages a compelling philosophy of excellent education and proof that this was possible even for children with disabilities and differences. Her story was the boost we needed in order to keep going amidst learning challenges. In addition to "dialoguing" with Cheryl throughout the chapters of her book, we have also benefitted from the *Simply Classical Journal* and forum,[5] both serving as resources for parents endeavoring to classically educate children with special needs. During a particularly challenging season, I reached out to Cheryl personally on the Simply Classical forum and received a thorough, articulate response with numerous suggestions for action. My surprise quickly turned to encouragement as I read her response, overwhelmed by profound gratitude for an experienced voice willing to speak into our situation.

We all need a "coach" in this long run toward reading. A good coach can be a vision specialist, psychologist, master teacher, educational therapist, or even an experienced friend. At times, you may even benefit from an entire coaching team comprised of helpful voices from different parts of your learning community! Regardless of their area of specialty, the best coaches offer a potent combination of knowledge,

4. Cheryl Swope, *Simply Classical: A Beautiful Education for Any Child*, 2nd ed. (Louisville: Memoria Press, 2019).

5. Access *Simply Classical Journal* and forum at www.memoriapress.com.

experience, confidence, and outside-of-the-box thinking. Perhaps most importantly, many of these coaches have crossed the finish line with another student before yours, adding the assets of empathy and perspective to their qualifications. If you find yourself in a place of loneliness and isolation, without a "coach" in sight, don't despair. The world is full of people who care deeply about your child and your family; you only have to find them. If you're still searching for an expert that will help see you through your training course, consider looking in some unconventional places—books, journal articles, blog posts, podcasts, and videos—until you find someone closer to home. Reach out to school counselors, doctor's offices, community organizations, church ministries, and even friends. You might be surprised to find that others around you are already training for the same goal!

FINDING A "COACH":
QUESTIONS TO CONSIDER

1. Does this person exhibit a depth of knowledge in his or her field (often—but not always—evidenced by academic degrees, training certificates, or professional endorsements)?

2. Does he or she offer the perspective of having helped students with similar problems?

3. Is he or she willing to help you pursue the kind of education you want for your child?

4. Is this person willing to consider the whole picture of your child—personality traits, medical history, emotional health, academic challenges, behavioral issues—in an effort to help you chart a path forward?

5. Does this person communicate effectively with you *and* your child? Is he or she willing to be part of a team effort, cooperating with others (medical professionals, teachers, counselors, etc.), as needed?

Gathering the Right Equipment

It came as no surprise to me that one of the most important pieces of equipment I needed as a novice runner was a good pair of shoes. However, I had no idea just how many options existed! Magazines, websites, and brick-and-mortar stores offer no shortage of shoe selection for runners of all shapes and sizes. The myriad options can be dizzying for someone new to the sport. After reading and researching and trying on an embarrassing number of shoes, I finally settled on the right pair for my body mechanics and mileage goals. The argument could be made that any sneaker will do, but my particular goal necessitated finding a shoe that would survive the many miles of marathon training and help me cross the finish line. I needed a shoe I could run in for a long time. And I certainly found one—I've been running in the same model for more than twenty years!

In the long run to reading, it's equally important to find quality "equipment" that you can use with some longevity. Finding materials that suit your child's reading needs and personality will enable him to make steady progress. However, switching curricula frequently can inhibit the kind of progress you are seeking. Don't rush your choice; take time to enlist the help of your coach, evaluate your options, and choose a suitable program that you can stick with.

When we first began addressing our child's reading needs, we chose to modify aspects of the curriculum his school was using by color-coding word segments, enlarging print, and reducing the amount of text on a page. These modifications prompted small gains; however, over time, it became clear to us that we needed to find a reading program that would both complement our school's (classical) educational philosophy and instruction and offer our child multi-sensory, methodical, engaging lessons that would yield steady, measurable progress. We needed a reading program that was "explicit, systematic, incremental, and simple."[6] Explicit phonics instruction, accompanied by "extended practice with phonemically decodable texts,"[7] would provide a critical foundation for our child's sustained reading progress. After researching and comparing options and seeking confirmation from our "coach," we decided to begin All About Reading as soon as our son finished first grade.

In the following months, we not only utilized a specific reading curriculum aimed at the skills of decoding and comprehension, but we also incorporated the use of other valuable resources. Viewfinders and rulers helped highlight the texts we read and eliminate obstacles for reading. Games like *Swish, Jr.* and *Rush Hour* helped facilitate the practice of different visual skills necessary for recognizing and differentiating between letters, phonograms, and whole words. Activity books like *Visual Perceptual Skill Building*[8] offered opportunities for further perceptual skill development. And to fill our son's mind with exposure to language he might be missing as a struggling reader, audiobooks and read-alouds provided a steady backdrop of new vocabulary, engaging stories, and opportunities to broaden linguistic confidence.

In her book, *Proust and the Squid*, author Maryanne Wolf highlights the significance of a child's exposure to the language of ideas at a young age. She writes:

6. From Laura Tucker's session on teaching reading, Association of Classical Christian Schools national conference, June 12, 2019.

7. Joseph K. Torgesen, "Avoiding the Devastating Downward Spiral," American Federation of Teachers (AFT), Accessed October 11, 2022, https://www.aft.org/per iodical/american-educator/fall-2004/avoiding-devastating-downward-spiral.

8. Raya Burstein, *Visual Perceptual Skill Building: Book 1* (North Bend: The Critical Thinking Co., 1998) and *Visual Perceptual Skill Building: Book 2* (North Bend: The Critical Thinking Co., 2000).

Years ago, the cognitive scientist David Swinney helped uncover the fact that when we read a simple word like "bug," we activate not only the more common meaning (a crawling, six-legged creature), but also the bug's less frequent associations—spies, Volkswagens, and glitches in software. Swinney discovered that the brain doesn't just find one simple meaning for a word; instead it stimulates a veritable trove of knowledge about that word and the many words related to it. The richness of this semantic dimension of reading *depends on the riches we have already stored*, a fact with important and sometimes devastating developmental implications for our children. Children with a rich repertoire of words and their associations will experience any text or conversation in ways that are substantively different from children who do not have the same stored words and concepts.[9]

Struggling readers naturally take in fewer stories on their own because of the difficulty of the task. One of the most significant gifts you can give your struggling reader is to fill her mind with rich, engaging sentences and stories. Parents have a unique opportunity to place deposits into the bank of a child's mind—and watch those investments grow exponentially. Susan Wise Bauer defends the importance of this storage act: "Young children are described as sponges because they soak up knowledge. But there's another side to the metaphor. Squeeze a dry sponge, and nothing comes out. First the sponge has to be filled."[10]

Finding day-to-day lessons that will guide your student towards reading fluency is essential, but so is filling his mind with a treasury of words and stories that he will be able to draw from along the way. "Fill

9. Maryanne Wolf, *Proust and the Squid: The Story and Science of the Reading Brain* (New York: Harper Collins, 2007), 9; emphasis mine.

10. Susan Wise Bauer and Jesse Wise, *The Well-Trained Mind: A Guide to Classical Education at Home* (New York: W. W. Norton & Company, 2019), 21–22.

the sponge" full with language that will better equip your child to make gains in both reading fluency and comprehension. Read rich stories, poetry, and even non-fiction texts out loud to your struggling reader. Invite her into family discussions of varied topics at the dinner table. Attend theater productions, concerts, sermons, and lectures. Include him in family or classroom read-alouds of books above his skill level. Let her hear the rhythms and rhymes of well-crafted phrases, sentences, and stanzas. Consider utilizing audiobooks related to current areas of study in order to supply your child with content vocabulary. Give your student the gift of plentiful words; one day, you will see the reward!

Scheduling for Success

In addition to expert advice and the right equipment, a thoughtful schedule has served as an integral component of my training plan for every long-distance race I've ever run. Even after years of running, I still print out a blank calendar template, count a certain number of weeks backward from race day, and pencil in my mileage plans. I do this for several reasons. First, and quite simply, scheduling my calendar reminds me that I do indeed have a plan! It serves as a visual reminder that I have undertaken steps to facilitate movement toward my goal. During week one of my training, I only need to worry about my goals for that particular week. I've already thought about the necessary components of my training; there is no need to look nervously ahead. After years of experience, I know that the slow and steady build will lead me to the fitness level required for race day. Secondly, running isn't my life—I'm also a wife, mother, teacher, writer, and friend. One important benefit of my calendar is that my training has a scheduled limit. There are days when I run, and there are days when I rest. Both are important in order for me to cross the finish line at the end of my calendar and grow in other areas of my life. Finally, my running schedule reflects an understanding of best practices in training for a long-distance race. My mileage plans and days per week spent running are not based on a throw of dice; they're based on tested models that work. I can move through the weeks of my schedule with confidence, knowing that I have a solid, workable plan to help me achieve my race goals.

A solid, consistent schedule is a significant component of a workable plan for struggling readers. Most children with reading challenges need even more repetition than the average student,[11] yet they simultaneously burn out and feel overwhelmed in a smaller amount of time. The remedy for this from a scheduling perspective is to plan short lessons or practice times with great frequency. The creator of All About Reading suggests that students spend twenty minutes working through a lesson and twenty minutes reading (or being read to) for pleasure during each day of schooling. We don't always abide by this rule, but the principle has helped me to plan a limit to our lessons. It's more important for us to end on a positive note than to push until we reach burnout.

If you're trying to help a struggling reader outside of regular school hours, scheduling difficulties are compounded. Such students already exert extra energy focusing on learning tasks during the school day, and they often come home with homework that takes even longer to complete than it might for a more accomplished reader. Adding reading remediation or perceptual therapy exercises to an increasingly exhausting day may not seem realistic or even helpful. But you still have options.

If your child attends a local school, consider asking to pull her out for reading instruction each day. You can do the teaching yourself or hire someone else to do it on your behalf.[12] If it's possible to do

11. Pati Montgomery, Melody Ilk, and Louisa Cook Moats, *A Principal's Primer for Raising Reading Achievement* (Longmont: Camblum Learning Groups/Sopris Learning, 2013), 66.

12. Some programs, such as All About Reading, provide open-and-go resources

this during the child's normal reading time, that's ideal; but don't let it deter you if you need to pull him out during a different subject. Reading is a foundational skill that will facilitate your child's learning in numerous subject areas; making it a priority is reasonable.

If you can't pull your child out for reading instruction each day, and your child's weekdays are simply too full, consider thinking outside of the box about what you could accomplish on weekends, during breaks, or over the summer. I've often ended a school year discouraged about the reading progress we've made during a particular grade, only to remember that we still have nearly three full months of summer ready for the taking! A child's reading at the end of one school year doesn't define what his skill level will be when he begins the next one. Look for ways to make practice fun and engaging—your child might not even realize you are "summer schooling"!

Have Plan, Will Read

A quick glance at almost any article, book, or website geared towards novice runners will reveal the priority of a training plan. Just like a runner training for a new race goal, parents and teachers of struggling readers need a solid plan built on an honest evaluation of their student's abilities. As running coach Janet Hamilton reminds would-be athletes, "You have to start where you are, not where you think you should be."[13] Once you have an accurate view of your student's starting point, finding a coach, gathering the right equipment, and creating a

---

for parents to teach their own child. Others, such as the Barton Method, require a qualified tutor. Both of these programs are based on the Orton-Gillingham model which complements the classical approach to teaching reading!

13. "How to Start Running Today: A Beginner's Guide," *Runner's World*, January 18, 2022, https://www.runnersworld.com/uk/training/beginners/a772727/how -to-start-running-today/.

schedule will support your goal. With these tools within your reach, you're ready to start training!

Ch. 3 "Notes from the Trainer": A Few Questions & Answers from Dr. David Pierce, OD

What first steps would you recommend for parents seeking to honestly evaluate a child's reading problems?

The alphabet is a key diagnostic tool. Does the child know the alphabet? At what level does he know it? Can he recognize each letter individually? Can he visualize each letter when it is called out? Can he pick out the letters without singing the alphabet song? Can he recognize both uppercase *and* lowercase versions of the letter? These are important visual/auditory clues to consider; strong auditory and visual connections are important in mastering reading, writing, and spelling.

If a child cannot see a letter in his head, he will not be able to write it on paper. He may be able to draw letters, but if he fails to visualize the letters in his mind, he is not writing words. There must be visualization, not just oral recitation or drawing. Too many parents and teachers pound away at reading remediation programs without first ensuring that the foundational skill of visualization is in place.

If you can teach a child to visualize, then he can become a reader. If he can't visualize—if he can't see that picture of a letter or word in his head—his forward progression will stall. He will gain short-term memory at best, but not the long-term retention that is essential for a lifetime of reading.

What creative resources do you recommend for addressing reading skill deficiencies?

A favorite tool in our clinic is the alphabet banner—a simple banner constructed of letter cards strung along a wall. A therapist uses a wooden dowel to point to a letter card, and the child sings his ABCs up to that letter card, pointing physically to each letter that is sung. ("L,m,n" is not a single letter!) This builds auditory recognition, visual location, and motor skills—core skills necessary for moving ahead in reading.

Another helpful activity is to draw letters or shapes on a child's back, asking the child to verbally identify each one. This requires the child to visualize the letter form and then label it with a name. The multisensory approach ensures that letter learning includes important visual processing skills.

How much time should students spend on reading training—or on improving any visual processing skills?

Student engagement is an important indicator of how much time to spend on skill practice. If a child is not engaged, the time may be wasted. Pushing too hard will result in resistance, and negative adaptive behaviors will develop—ten good minutes are better than thirty unproductive ones.

Small bursts of skill practice allow time for the child to process what she has learned, an important factor in creating neurological connections. Frequent, successful repetition is required in order to undo old habits and form new ones!

It's also important to give these students time to process after a lesson or activity. If you don't allow enough processing time, then you reach an impasse, an "absorption level" that the child can't move past. There is no new space left for continued learning. Giving the child mental space beyond what was required of him in the lesson or activity provides him with the necessary time to digest new information and file it away for later use. He will then be ready to build further skills in the future. Failure to give adequate processing time often leads to emotional overwhelm and an inability to move forward with learning—additional obstacles best avoided.

Training for the Long Run

Summer was turning to fall, and my husband and I had signed up for a two-day, 25k/15k trail run through a local nature preserve. With our training schedule mapped out and newly purchased trail running shoes on our feet, we struck out on a short path recommended by a seasoned trail runner. Our goal was clear: acclimate to running on an ungroomed trail and finish the three-mile loop. At first, I was enamored by the scenery; running in the trees provided a wonderful respite from pounding the pavement at our local track. Fluttering leaves danced in the wind. Wildflower pockets and woodland animals provided a steady distraction. However, the high summer sun beat down in oppressive heat, and our forest run was far from flat. Soon I found myself breathing hard and willing my legs to climb each consecutive rock-strewn hill. Only halfway through our loop, I was already discouraged. How would I ever run this kind of terrain for twenty-five miles?

I silently preached to myself as I ran: *This is an achievable goal. My body can do this. It's only three miles; you run this distance all the time.* With my eyes trained on the ground in front of me—and a silent prayer for supernatural balance—I placed one foot in front of the other along the rugged path. My ankles wobbled as I leapt over boulders and tree roots. My body ached, and my confidence wavered, but I knew I had selected an appropriate goal. In truth—if not in reality—I had been here before; the first week is always the hardest. Our plan wasn't the problem; this was simply the hard work of getting stronger.

The First Mile

Strengthening a student's reading skill is a lot like strengthening any muscle in our bodies: it's uncomfortable—even painful—at first, but consistency and repetition increase our capabilities. The steady compilation of daily mental exercise yields improvement in reading. There is no substitute for simply *doing the work*; this may be one of the most challenging components of helping your struggling student.

Consulting with a coach, readying your equipment, and penning a schedule are necessary preparations, but they won't benefit you or your student if you never actually *begin training*. The unglamorous hours you and your child will spend strengthening her mental muscles are not the goal, of course—but they are the means of reaching it. The challenge for you and your child is to commit to the work and muster up the energy to engage each reading task.

Attending to the work may not seem difficult at first. Perhaps the excitement of a new strategy, the purchase of a new set of books, or inspiration from a beaming coach will carry you through the first few steps with zeal. Your child might even find easy success with his first few lessons or therapy sessions. Enjoy the thrill of achievement and praise your child, but don't be surprised if this spark quickly fades—and you find yourself wondering if your plan was doomed from the start. When that moment comes, be prepared to speak the truth to yourself and your child: mental fatigue and emotional exhaustion simply demonstrate that you are doing something difficult. You don't have to be excited about each step to be a good teacher, parent, or student; you need only *keep going*.

Pace Yourself

The pace of any training plan poses significant implications for achievement. An overemphasis on speed or an amount of ground to cover leads to burnout. However, a lax pace requiring little effort will yield little progress. Steady effort results in long-term reward. In short, the pace of every workout matters—for readers as well as runners.

When I first began running in college, I sought the company of a friend for my daily training runs. With a small pool of interested parties, I heartily welcomed anyone who was willing to join me. One particularly sunny afternoon, I struck out on a familiar route with a strong, long-legged friend. We followed my usual path, stopped to stretch, and then continued down a deserted country road. In my mind, it was a perfect plan—a good run with good company. However, I soon realized that I had failed to consider a significant factor in the success of our endeavor: the pace. I struggled to breathe while keeping up with the flash of legs in front of me, certain that my very tall friend was striving to hold herself back on my account. My feet grabbed at patches of pavement in vain; I simply couldn't keep up. Our bodies were not a good match, and the end result of our efforts was neither enjoyable nor motivating for either of us.

While there is an appropriate place for speed workouts in an athlete's training, most experts recommend that the bulk of running follow a pace that allows a person to carry on a conversation. The ability to do so demonstrates that the body isn't being overtaxed. For long-distance runners, this is especially important: "A common mistake among novice endurance athletes is when they notice they are feeling good early in a long race, they start moving faster, only to implode in the later miles. Veteran athletes, on the other hand, know the importance of showing restraint, even—and perhaps especially—when things are going well. *You've got to go slow to go fast.*[1]

Reading remediation requires the same strategy: we have to go slow (appropriately pace each lesson) to go fast (achieve reading fluency). As a teacher, I encounter the same temptation to ignore the importance of pace during reading lessons. At times, I'm tempted to push my student quickly through a lesson or text in an effort to check it off our "to do" list or to "make more progress" (a phrase self-defeating enough by itself). The allure of catching up with peers or finally reading at grade level is ever present. However, such motives nearly always produce the same result: an initial burst of energy—usually incited by the presence of a jellybean bribe—followed by sudden fatigue, noticeable discouragement, and eventual shut-down. Progress is nowhere to be found. In contrast, when teachers move at a speed that strikes the balance between challenging and attainable, a child proceeds with confidence and finishes with a sense of accomplishment. Not only does the student *progress* that day, but he ends with a positive view towards the next learning task—and the next, and the next. On a journey that will consist of weeks and years of attentiveness and engagement, neither teachers nor students can afford to burn out on day one.

When your child's "reading workouts" begin, consider *daily pace* (how much you pursue in one practice session) in addition to the pacing of your overall schedule (your long-term weekly, monthly, or yearly plan). Either you or your child might be tempted to attack the first practice sessions with unusual vigor. Harness that energy for days ahead,

---

1. Brad Stulberg, "What We Can Learn from Endurance Athletes about Getting Through This Pandemic," *The New York Times*, May 21, 2020, https://www.nytimes .com/2020/05/21/well/mind/coronavirus-athletes-marathons-triathlons-sports -cycling.html. (emphasis mine)

remembering that an overemphasis on speed will ultimately yield a decrease in both progress and motivation. To determine if your pacing is appropriate, think about your current training: Does your student struggle to remember rules or skills learned in a previous lesson? Do you routinely skip warm-up or review, immediately asking your child to pursue a new skill during each reading session? At the end of a lesson, does your student show visible signs of exhaustion and burnout? Do you repeatedly find yourself frustrated and angry that you didn't progress as far as you hoped in a lesson? Do you regularly spend more time on reading lessons than most experts suggest? If you answered "yes" to any of these questions, consider slowing your pace. Moving too fast will lead to initially hopeful practice sessions ending with discouragement, and your child feeling the weight of failure when, in reality, he is moving on a steady trajectory towards improvement. These are unnecessary hindrances in an already difficult journey. The reward of appropriate pacing is well worth the effort required to sustain it. Remember, helping a struggling reader is *a marathon, not a sprint!*

In addition to facilitating progress in reading instruction, appropriately paced lessons also give your student a framework for pacing his or her own independent reading later on. *Slow* isn't just the antonym of *fast*; it's a method for approaching a text. Taking the time to prepare for (pre-reading), read, and comprehend (post-reading/reflection) a long or complicated text requires time; it cannot be rushed. Working through such a text too quickly will yield only a cursory level of comprehension at best—or misunderstanding at worst. Slow reading leads to a deeper, more thorough understanding and appreciation of a text. Especially for students who come to the reading life with exceptional challenges, slow reading is an important skill to hone.[2]

2. Andrea Lipinski and Andrew Kern's *A Guide to Reading* (Concord: CiRCE Institute, 2017) offers one way to engage in slow reading: a layered approach. James W. Sire's *How to Read Slowly: Reading for Comprehension* (Colorado Springs: Waterbrook Press, 1989) provides guidance for slow reading across genres.

Read. Then Repeat.

Repetition and consistency are the building blocks for strengthening most any skill. Reading expert Dr. Sally Shaywitz affirms the importance of regular reading practice: "New brain imaging technology shows the powerful positive effect of practice in creating neural circuits related to the development of what scientists call expertise or skill. Basically, the brain learns by practice."[3] Numerous scientific studies offer insight into the strengthening of neural pathways through consistent reading practice. One study from the University of Washington concludes that "targeted, intensive reading programs not only lead to substantial improvements in reading skills, but also change the underlying wiring of the brain's reading circuitry."[4]

A clinical study from the Center for Cognitive Brain Imaging at Carnegie Mellon University reinforces this observation. Researchers studied the neurological effects of one hundred hours of targeted reading remediation on a group of eight- to ten-year-old children. Specifically, they sought evidence of a change in white matter, part of the brain "which lies beneath the gray matter cortex, [and] is composed of millions of bundles of axons (nerve fibers) that connect neurons in different brain regions into functional circuits."[5] According to the study, "the instruction resulted in a change in white matter . . . correlated with improvement in phonological decoding ability, clarifying

---

3. Sally Shaywitz, *Overcoming Dyslexia: A New and Complete Science-Based Program for Reading Problems at Any Level* (New York: Vintage, 2005), 188.

4. University of Washington, "How Instruction Changes Brain Circuitry with Struggling Readers," ScienceDaily, June 14, 2018, www.sciencedaily.com/releases/2018/06/180614213556.htm.

5. R. Douglas Fields, "Change in the Brain's White Matter," *Science* 330 (Nov. 5, 2010): 768–69, accessed February 2, 2023, https://www.ncbi.nlm.nih.gov/pmc/articles/PMC3201847/.

the cognitive locus of the effect. The results demonstrate the capability of a behavioral intervention to bring about a positive change in cortico-cortical white matter tracts."[6] In other words, reading training yields real neurological change!

If our goal as parents and teachers of struggling readers is to increase the development of neural pathways and train the brain to read, how does one go about accomplishing such a task? The answer is simple to identify, yet sometimes difficult to implement: consistent repetition and practice. Just as learning math facts facilitates forward movement in mathematics, reading has its own set of components to acquire. Initially, a student must practice identifying the names and sounds of individual letters. Learning phonograms and decoding rules soon follows, accompanied by an awareness of linguistic patterns that will aid in reading fluency. While this progression seems simple enough, it can be painfully slow for some students. Slow processing speed, working memory deficits, or low self-confidence—any number of interfering disabilities, disorders, or differences[7]—may land a student at the early stages of sound-to-symbol identification for months. In fact, training a student with dyslexia or another learning disability requires 40–200 times more repetition than training the average student does.[8] If this is where you find yourself, don't despair. There is no time clock on the race to reading fluency.

6. Timothy A. Keller and Marcel Adam Just, "Altering Cortical Connectivity: Remediation-Induced Changes in the White Matter of Poor Readers," *Neuron* 64/5 (Dec. 10, 2009): 624–31, see especially p. 624, accessed February 2, 2023, https://www.sciencedirect.com/science/article/pii/S0896627309008472.

7. See Susan Wise Bauer's book *Rethinking School: How to Take Charge of Your Child's Education* (New York: W. W. Norton, 2018) for a helpful discussion of the distinctions between disabilities and differences.

8. Pati Montgomery, Melody Ilk, and Louisa Cook Moats, *A Principal's Primer for Raising Reading Achievement* (Longmont: Camblum Learning Groups/Sopris Learning, 2013), 66.

Mindful of Mystery

I can recall days upon days of shuffling through the same phonogram cards with my child. Months into taking over his reading instruction, I sometimes wondered if I had gotten the plan terribly wrong—some days, he could identify the sounds of the letters on the phonogram cards, and some days he stared at me in silence. Was there a key to deciphering this pattern? Over time, I developed a sense for possible contributors to this enigmatic phenomenon (fatigue, emotional distractions, illness), but part of the experience remains a mystery. Human beings are complex creatures, comprised of more than mere neurological impulses firing—or misfiring—on command. Awareness of this truth offers more than a justifiable defense for unanswered questions; it shapes good pedagogy.

The best strategies and methods bump up against the boundaries of human nature. Any parent knows this well; who among us hasn't wondered *where did this child come from?!* A child's passions and tendencies may be altogether unlike his mother's or father's. Her creativity may masquerade as disconnection or distraction. His personality might seem different from anyone else in the family tree. Her way of working, studying, or problem-solving may appear backward or haphazard compared to your way of seeing the world. As parents and teachers, we tend to teach the way that *we* learn best; we plan our trajectories in a way that makes sense to *us*. Yet it is often when we remember that we all reflect the image of God differently—in glorious, yet sometimes irritating ways! —that we best serve our struggling students.

Teaching from a place of humility and wonder, we acquire a perspective of human nature that allows for uniqueness, imagination, and difference. We acknowledge that the co-labor of learning necessarily involves an element of mystery. German philosopher Joseph Pieper articulates this facet of the human experience:

> Wonder signifies that the world is profounder, more all-embracing and mysterious than the logic of everyday reason had taught us to believe. The innermost meaning of wonder is fulfilled in a deepened sense of mystery. It does not end in doubt, but is the awakening of the knowledge that being, *qua* being, is mysterious and inconceivable, and that it is a mystery in the full sense of the word: neither a dead end, nor a contradiction, nor even something impenetrable in the dark. Rather, mystery means that a reality cannot be comprehended *because* its light is ever-flowing, unfathomable, and inexhaustible. And that is what the wonderer really experiences.[9]

Such has been the case in our reading journey: we wonder at the enigma of human learning. While moments of mystery have tempted me toward frustration and discouragement, they have also served as reminders that I am teaching a unique person—a human being whose mind, at times, leads me to wonder. And I choose, like Aristotle, to believe that "out of wonder . . . comes joy."[10] Trusting our coach and other expert voices, and committed to the task of learning, we simply press on towards our goal—day after day, week after week, month after month—with consistent repetition. The remarkable result? Progress! It's difficult to achieve this perspective in the midst of the daily grind of phonics lessons and read-alouds, but day after day of repetition

9. Joseph Pieper, *Leisure: The Basis of Culture* (San Fransisco: Ignatius Press, 2009), 115.

10. Aristotle, as quoted in Pieper, *Leisure*, 117.

and practice is building skill your struggling reader needs in order to pursue the reading life.

Adding Miles

The best curricula will slowly and methodically add to a foundation already laid, but these new steps often feel more like giant leaps for a student with reading challenges. Acquiring new reading skill necessitates energy and effort; students must exercise attention and focus before new concepts become automatic. In the time between the first step and automaticity, the training simply feels *hard*. The good news is that once those new skills are internalized, a reader will read the concept with relative ease. He will look back on those earlier-learned skills the same way I reflect on a seven-mile run during long-distance race training—at first, painful and laborious, but that's because my body wasn't yet conditioned for the task. With time and repetition, what seems insurmountable becomes a new foundation, laying the groundwork for further progress.

When I begin training for a long-distance race, I aim to lengthen my longest run incrementally, usually just a mile or two each week. The weekly increase in mileage is only slight, but its effects can be staggering—literally! On the day of one such recent increase, I was jogging my normal distance down a familiar dirt road when my muscles began to stiffen. I had moved past my usual mental mile markers . . . *one mile at the first bend, one mile at the waterfall, one mile at the field crossing* . . . before consulting my GPS to find the end of the last remaining mile. My eyes blinked in disbelief; I couldn't believe how slowly the numbers were changing! Despite the seemingly slight increase in distance, each minute seemed to require the effort of an hour. Why did it feel so much harder?

"Adding mileage" in reading induces similar effects of bewilderment and exhaustion. Learning new concepts and acquiring new skills takes extraordinary effort for children with special needs. Planning days to "take the mileage down" can help prevent overwhelm and increase motivation for pressing on. For example, most of the focused phonics lessons in All About Reading are followed by a story which requires the student to put her newfound knowledge and skill into practice. This encourages students to internalize new rules and apply them in a functional context. Reading these new, more difficult stories necessitates a different kind of effort and focus than stories illustrating already acquired concepts—and this energy and focus often results in fatigue. When my reader-in-training appears especially fatigued from applying new concepts, we opt to reread a story or play a review game before pressing onward. The act of repeating an already read text has pedagogical benefit in and of itself,[11] but such a task also offers my student a chance to catch his breath before heading up the next hill.

The Mental Game

The mind-body connection has drastic implications for endurance training. Long-distance pursuits require more than just a commitment to action. A plethora of books, magazines, and websites dedicated to helping long-distance runners achieve their goals reveals that the actual physical work of running isn't always the obstacle that inhibits an athlete's training. In fact, some postulate that "the mental challenge of long runs and races can be just as tough (if not more difficult) as the

---

11. For a discussion of the benefits of repeated reading exercises for reading fluency, see Leah Zimmermann and Deborah K. Reed, "Repeated Reading with Goal Setting for Reading Fluency: Focusing on Reading Quality Instead of Reading Speed," Iowa Reading Research Center, February 5, 2019, https://iowareadin gresearch.org/blog/repeated-reading-fluency.

[physical] demands of the distance."[12] Experts suggest that "psychological factors ... have a direct effect on the decision to stop [physical exercise]."[13] Distance, pace, discomfort, and environmental factors all contribute to runner burnout.[14] In other words, long-distance running is a bit of a mind game: what happens in the head affects what the limbs are willing to do.

Struggling students experience the same mental struggle in the long-range endeavor of learning to read. Skill acquisition and practice often extend past weeks and months into years (distance, pace). Oftentimes the act of reading causes physical strain and fatigue (discomfort). Certainly, excessive heat or cold, noisy surroundings, or an uncomfortable room (environment) can cause distraction from the reading task. The good news is that these obstacles are not insurmountable, but conquering them requires an awareness of our human makeup. Just like runners, readers are *whole people*, whose thoughts, feelings, and even physical sensations cannot be compartmentalized. What we *think* invariably affects how we *feel*, and how we *feel* has drastic implications for how we *act*. This is true for all learners, but students with special needs encounter these challenges in extraordinary ways. Students with drifting eyes feel the increased physical strain of eye focus during daily reading sessions. Children with behavioral challenges battle for mental focus and fight their way through distractions during each lesson. Learners with emotional disorders struggle to give their feelings appropriate value and pursue new concepts with confidence. A wise teacher will consider the effects of such pressures on a student's

12. Christine Luff, "Mind Games for Long Runs and Races," Run for Good, July 20, 2022, http://run-for-good.com/mind-games-for-long-runs-and-races/.

13. Mariska Van Sprundel, "Running and the Science of Mental Toughness," The *MIT Press Reader*, MIT Press, accessed October 8, 2022, https://thereader.mitpress.mit.edu/running-and-the-science-of-mental-toughness/.

14. Ibid.

stamina. A holistic view of your student offers insight for supporting him in the pursuit of the reading life.

Addressing Both Body & Mind

Many of the same strategies distance runners use to overcome mental hurdles can be employed by struggling readers and their teachers in order to promote reading progress. Before a long training run or race even begins, experts suggest that runners "dress for success" and maintain a body position of confidence. For readers, we could call this physical readiness and posture. Being physically prepared for a task affects mental inclination. Body posture plays a critical role in reading; it affects attitude, physical engagement, and even cognitive function. While striking a particular pose for a runner may signal confidence to the brain, the effect of a reader's posture extends beyond that. An upright position can signal an attitude of optimism; research suggests it can even contribute to a higher processing speed.[15] If your student prefers to lay in a beanbag or sit at a half-recline at his desk during lessons, consider inviting him to sit up tall and breathe deeply before beginning his reading practice.

Another strategy for runners mentally overwhelmed by the volume of their training is to break long runs up into smaller increments and focus on completing each "bite-sized" goal, one at a time, until the greater distance is finished. We do this often with reading lessons, especially those involving a story of considerable length. My student regularly counts the pages of a story to gauge where he is in the process and how much text remains to be read. We often set a goal of just a

---

15. Sarah Awad, Tobias Debatin, and Albert Ziegler, "Embodiment: I Sat, I Felt, I Performed—Posture Effects on Mood and Cognitive Performance," *Acta Psychologica* 218 (2021): 103353.

few pages before taking a break and continuing on. This coping strategy is backed up by science: In 2010, Samuele Marcora conducted a study that required athletes to pedal an exercise bike for as long as they could manage, without any particular time as a goal. (For interested parties, the average ride lasted just twelve minutes.) "It was the final part of the test that proved most interesting. After the endurance test the scientists asked the athletes to . . . [complete a] five-second explosive burst of cycling. . . . [T]he men . . . generate[d] three times more power than they had during the longer endurance test."[16] The athletes knew they only had to push for five seconds! The study concluded that "tired muscles and a lack of energy [were] not the problem."[17] A lack of a clear end-point dealt the mental blow that led to burnout in the endurance test. In contrast, during the five-second challenge, the athletes' minds were focused on the short-term goal rather than their perception of effort. Their performance indicates that they were willing to work harder because the end was in sight.

You can help your reader endure long training days, weeks, and months by breaking necessary work up into more palatable chunks. While a lesson may not be finished or a concept mastered in the time you have allotted, giving your child a clear stopping point is critical for encouraging optimal performance during reading sessions. Not only will this motivate your student's mind for one day's reading task, it will build confidence and optimism for facing the next one.

Managing Your Environment

In addition to her own body, a runner's training environment significantly affects her mental focus. Since I do the majority of my running

16. Van Sprundel, "Running and the Science of Mental Toughness."
17. Ibid.

outdoors, seasonal shifts play a large role in creating the backdrop for my training runs. At the start of the year, most of my training takes place mid-day so as to avoid the coldest temperatures of morning and evening. I dress in layers, take my time warming up, and watch for patches of slippery ice and snow on the trail. My winter runs are shorter because there is less daylight, and when the sun goes down, so does my energy level! When spring comes, I battle the stress of end-of-semester job responsibilities and end-of-school activities for my children, leaving me precious little time to weave running in between seasonal downpours. Summer offers more free time and flexibility, but it's accompanied by scorching heat that necessitates planning early morning runs and an ample water supply. Fall is my favorite time for long-distance running. The heat begins to die down, but the days are still long, offering plenty of time and sunshine to accomplish all of my daily tasks, running included. October ushers in brilliant turquoise skies and the slight morning chill that tells of change. By early November, as I'm often wrapping up training for a long-distance trail race, the temperature is cool and the forests ablaze with color, painting a glorious backdrop for my zealous romp through the local nature preserve in pursuit of my year-end goals.

With the seasonal changes in temperature and surroundings, my training runs exhibit different needs. In particularly busy seasons, I'm mindful of how stress and/or fatigue affect my body and ability to train. In the high heat of summer, shade and water are non-negotiables. In winter, forgetting an extra layer can spell misery—or even injury. And sometimes I need to adjust the time of day for my training runs to accommodate daylight or weather shifts. As in all human pursuits, flexibility is key, as our bodies are home to our minds. We are whole people, and what happens to part of us affects the rest of us, perhaps more than we are often willing to admit.

During the hard work of reading training, don't forget to consider how your child's environment, health, and other life stressors might be affecting his performance. A fight with a sibling, a difficult math test, hunger or thirst, excessive heat or cold, and even darkness or light can distract a student's focus from fully engaging in the training task at hand. Many struggling students are highly sensitive to noise and need a quiet, private setting for working. Sally Shaywitz argues that "the necessity of devoting all of his attention to decoding the words on the page makes a dyslexic reader extremely vulnerable to any noises or movements. Reading for him is fragile, and the process can be disrupted at any moment."[18] As your student's guide, seek to protect her delicate learning environment. Strive to be a keen observer of the whole picture of her learning context. Providing a comfortable, distraction-free space for learning liberates your student from emotional and environmental deterrents to focus her efforts on the real work at hand—learning to read.

A Persistent Presence

While we may not have ultimate control over issues such as fatigue, illness, friendships, or weather patterns, parents and teachers *can* make an effort to mitigate such distractions that may hinder the hard work of reading training. If providing an extra snack or moving your training session to daylight hours eases tension and promotes learning, go for it! Ultimately, your student must do the daily work, but as a parent or teacher, you have the power to shape the learning process for good. Don't discount the role you have been given; your persistent presence is a constant reminder that all of this training is headed somewhere, and the destination is worth the journey.

18. Shaywitz, *Overcoming Dyslexia*, 116.

Warning: Training Will Change You

Teaching a child with a significant difference or disability to read is most definitely a journey—a set of adventures that leads to incredible change. However, sometimes that change isn't what we expect. We anticipate the hard work of reading training to shape a student's ability, but no less will it change *the student*. After years of watching my struggling student grow in both skill and character, it's difficult to discern which is more critical for a lifetime of reading success. Attending to daily lessons, learning to ban distractions, and focusing on a (mentally *and* physically) difficult task doesn't just produce reading fluency; it produces character. In the years we've been engaged in focused reading remediation and visual skill building, my struggling student has grown in determination, discipline, fortitude, and independence. He is not the child he once was—and this is not primarily owing to a particular reading skill. Years of climbing over hurdles and knocking down barriers have left him changed. Such formative work is the product of a greater power: "suffering produces endurance, and endurance produces character, and character produces hope."[19] Despite the difficulty—or perhaps *because* of it? —my young reader radiates a kind of hope that only comes out of a refining fire.

While I may not have anticipated my child's character formation as a result of reading training, I was even less prepared to encounter my own. Yet the truth is clear: helping to hoist my child over hurdles and laboring alongside him to chip away at barriers has led to my own transformation. Hours of teaching, prodding, and waiting have borne witness to both motherly love and human selfishness: while the former compels me, the latter constrains me. Every day I make

19. Romans 5:3–4, (ESV).

the choice anew—to press on or to give up. Yet with every "yes" to a reading lesson, homework session, or bedtime story, I stomp down the weeds along the path of leadership a little more, and the dirt becomes a trail. I grow in commitment, focus, and servanthood. I practice the discipline of dying to self. I see with more empathy and am less apt to offer judgment. I am patient in ways I never thought possible. It's not just my child who has changed; this fellowship of long-term labor has shaped me, and I too am not who I once was.

No Longer the Same

I remember the young, untested excitement of signing up for my first long-distance race. I had joy and energy on my side, and maybe even a dose of personal discipline. Even so, I am not the runner I once was. Hours and hours of running have cultivated a different kind of perspective: I have different kinds of goals; I've learned I can't outpace injury; I know my mileage schedule affects others; I recognize that I have limits, some of which I voluntarily place on myself. Today, increases in mileage don't require any less effort—perhaps they require *more* with each passing year—but the pile of long runs I've accumulated over the last two decades has made me tougher, stronger, more disciplined. Today, what I lack in strength or speed I make up for with an aged fortitude. It's a confidence amassed through years of training. If in my twenties I ran with youthful curiosity, today I run with seasoned *hope*—"and hope does not disappoint."

CH. 4 "NOTES FROM THE TRAINER": A FEW QUESTIONS & ANSWERS FROM DR. DAVID PIERCE, OD

In your experience, what keeps students/families from beginning the work of visual skill building and reading remediation?

Parents of struggling readers simply don't know where to begin. The majority of parents I see have tried too many strategies with no success. No parent or teacher is handed a manual for exactly how to alleviate their child's weaknesses; most times parents just don't know what to do. If they have a very different way of processing information than their child (which is oftentimes the case!), the frustration is compounded. The number one comment I get from parents whose children I've helped build visual skill is, "Thank you for helping me understand my child and find the tools to help him."

Without a well-balanced auditory-visual system, a struggling reader can't move forward. He can only achieve short-term memory; he can't build long-term retention. The task for parents is to learn their child's processing style—how she thinks—and her learning problems—the specific missing skills inhibiting her progress. In my practice, 99 percent of children I evaluate demonstrate a problem with visualization. The child has learned a coping skill that helps her cope with a dysfunctional visual system.

In addition to not knowing where to begin or how to help, the emotional burden of caring for a struggling child often overwhelms parents at the beginning of this type of journey. As time passes, parents learn to adjust to their child and acquire new tools for building skills. But at the beginning of a long road, the fear and frustration can be suffocating—and sometimes paralyzing.

You often have students practice visual skills at home as well as in your office setting. How important is practice (repetition and consistency) for strengthening reading skills?

One hour a week in my office isn't enough to make reading "click." Perceptual therapy sessions help parents understand their child more and learn tools for skill building, but they aren't magical. The hours of work that happen outside of the office are critical for a child's reading success.

I only accept clients whose parents are willing to work with their child outside of weekly therapy sessions. Each of these families commits to four practice days outside of their weekly office visit. Parents need to learn their child's processing struggles, and I help them do that. However, I can't create understanding and help a child build skill without parents engaging in the work. Visual and perceptual skill building requires regular repetition and consistency that works together to form a functional system. When families commit to that work, the results are amazing; however, without parent involvement, my clients—even those with bright potential—will see little progress.

What principles help you guide the pace of a student's training work?

For most of my clients, "I can't" means "give me more time." When the element of speed is removed from the reading equation and we patiently wait for indications of understanding or response, the most reluctant readers make progress. This principle should inform the bulk of your instruction. However, for a student to learn to function in academic environments where timing is sometimes required, it's helpful to add timed elements to therapy, little by little.

Timed tasks necessitate an awareness of how to do things. A timed test is not about a child's intelligence, but about how well he performs under pressure. Incorporating short bursts of speed drills periodically is important. Do a little speed work, then back off. Speed shouldn't be the main goal, but it should be included as a part of training.

It's important for a child to see elements of success and to have time to grab hold of that. Give space after learning for a child to process information and sense success. For example, I often use color-coded word family cards to do speed drills with children. Clients are often wary of this type of task, initially. However, when they realize that they can understand a pattern and read these words quickly (often as the result of the color-coding!), an awareness of success breaks through, and they discover that such tasks are possible!

CHAPTER FIVE

The Magic of Motivation

While many of my training miles and most of my running goals reach their fulfillment in the fall, it's no coincidence that summer is when motivation is on my mind. School is out—both for the kids and for my husband and me—and we lose the predictable rhythm of workdays and weekends. There are more mouths at home all day to feed, six different schedules to manage, and few pockets of time with enough supervisory care for me to slip out for a run. When that somewhat elusive window does pop up, I am often tired or preoccupied—or it may be 104 degrees outside. (Does anyone want to run in 104 degrees?!)

Without adequate motivation, training stops and goals collapse. I don't have to keep working the same exact plan to keep running, but I can't stop altogether and expect to reach my finish line. Honesty and flexibility are key; I must reorient to the challenges in front of me and find ways to push through the haze until I can see my goal with clarity once again.

Perhaps unsurprisingly, one such summer running slump happened to coincide with hitting a wall in our summer reading plans at home. Having completed the last reading level with my son before our two-week vacation, my goal had been to resume our lessons right away and hopefully avoid the "summer slide."[1] But it wasn't that easy. Unlike our tutoring sessions during the school year, *everyone* was home, and the house was filled with noise and distraction. In addition to the inhospitable environment for reading sessions, my husband was teaching a summer class, another child was sick, and I was the sole driver available for carting everyone else to and from summer jobs and activities. In summary: it wasn't working.

My son's motivation decreased by the day. When we finally did sit down to the first lesson in our new reading level, I wondered how we had lost so much steam. I was faced with a choice: power through and force our way back into a routine (was that even possible?) or take some time to tend to our motivational needs before pressing on towards progress (would we fizzle out altogether?). I closed the glossy cover on my new teacher's manual and set it aside before sending my son after his favorite series of readers—a set of sixteen books about dog breeds.[2] The books matched his reading capabilities and would serve as an engaging review; he loved anything having to do with dogs!

An enticing text wasn't enough to pull us back on track at first, so I dangled the carrot of screen time (which we generally limit) as a reward for finishing a book and broke our reading sessions up into small chunks interspersed with breaks. In a matter of days, our routine shifted from regular standoffs over reading to my son hunting me down every morning with a new dog breed book in hand. In a relatively short amount of time, my child's attitude had been transformed, all owing to fresh incentives: he had a measurable goal (read one reader per day), a short-term reward (screen time), an engaging text (on his

1. The phrase "summer slide" refers to a downward trajectory in skill building and retention over the summer months when students are typically away from formal instruction.

2. Sara Green, Dog Breeds series (Minnetonka, MN: Bellwether Media, 2011).

favorite subject—dogs), and a routine that took his current stamina into account (increasing reading time slowly instead of pushing towards burnout). The wonderful result? Motivation!

For parents and teachers of struggling students, an unwavering belief in the importance and impact of a reading life serves as sufficient motivation for the work ahead of us, but our students don't normally begin in the same place. They struggle to catch a vision for working towards a far-off goal. For them, the task is hard and the finish line is far away, separated by a canyon of questions and uncertainty. Our students may not have yet tasted the fruits of the reading life that will convince them of its value, but numerous methods for motivation are available to coax them toward this end.

Short-Term Reward

Outfitted with sticker charts, classroom bar graphs, and jars filled with cotton balls, primary schools across the nation testify to the effectiveness of the incremental reward. At their best, these tools both lure students toward a goal with an immediate, short-term reward (for example, learning all of the multiplication facts for a particular numeral) *and* move them toward a long-term goal of achievement (perhaps mastering *all* of the multiplication facts for numbers 0 to 12). Both types of rewards—immediate and long-term—are useful for student motivation and progress. Especially for younger children, incentivizing only long-term success isn't enough to gain student attention and effort; struggling students are likely to burn out before they reach the reward. Short-term incentives entice students to apply themselves to the tasks at hand *daily*, and it is this daily (or regular) work that moves struggling students along the continuum of skill development.

For our family, short-term rewards have taken various forms. When my son was young, and the work was most difficult, I rewarded correct phonogram or word pronunciation with a single M&M candy. We piled them into a bowl throughout our lesson, and my son was allowed to gobble them up at the end of each tutoring session. As his reading progressed, the rewards shifted a bit, but I still offered short-term incentives: a jellybean per line of text or page of a story, a pack of gummy bears for finishing a particularly difficult daily lesson, and sometimes coins or even a dollar bill for pushing through a difficult practice session. Our reading binder contains a page for marking each completed lesson with a sticker, but oftentimes we have not completed a full lesson each day, leaving no visible short-term reward for real work and progress. While choosing four or five jellybeans from an organized tray of flavors may not seem like an important ritual, it reminds my struggling reader that his effort is valuable, even when we don't complete a whole lesson in our curriculum

Of course, immediate rewards need not always involve sugar (although it does appear to be an effective aid!). Our reading instruction has been scattered with various other short-term incentives as well, such as sending a reading video to a classroom teacher, visiting a grandparent to share progress, spending a few minutes snuggling a pet, or even sharing important milestones with peers in a class. The point of a short-term reward is that your student associates the incentive with the immense value of putting in effort on a regular basis. Short-term rewards will serve you both well as you look forward to long-term gains.

The Races Along the Way

While marathon and ultra-marathon runners clearly have "the big one" in mind during training, you might be surprised to discover that many of these athletes cross the finish lines of other, shorter races along the way. These "tune-up races" serve a variety of purposes:

they reward training progress, provide a pause for assessment, develop confidence, and provide a physiological boost.[3] Weeks of training are rewarded with a fun venue, an energetic community, and even achievement medals! Tune-up races also provide an opportunity to take stock of where you are as a runner—the strengths and weaknesses exhibited in your race trial—and calculate any necessary training adjustments. Mentally, these races can provide a boost of confidence, a physical reminder that a runner is becoming stronger and more capable.

In many ways, we've treated the completion of a reading level like crossing the finish line of a tune-up race in our journey to reading fluency. Each student book in our reading program includes a certificate of achievement—a tangible reward that marks a milestone in my child's training, much like a finisher's medal at the end of a 5k. In addition to the certificate, we present our student with a significant gift to mark his achievement; this celebration acknowledges both the effort that has led him to this point and the worthiness of the work that lies ahead of us. The end of each reading level (culminating after anywhere from six to twelve months), like the finish line of a tune-up run, offers us a noticeable opportunity to pause and reflect on our gains and losses, our strengths and weaknesses. We often recognize methods and activities that have been helpful in the process, and sometimes we note aspects of our training that need to change. Regardless of what our end-of-level reflections and assessments yield in terms of strategy, taking the time to mark the accomplishment promotes gratitude and builds confidence. We remember, and then we ready ourselves for the task of training again, fixing our eyes on the finish line ahead of us.

---

3. Laura Norris, "How to Include TuneUp Races in Your Training," *Laura Norris Running*, accessed October 8, 2022, https://lauranorrisrunning.com/tune-up-races/.

Milestones

As you move along the path to reading fluency with your struggling reader, you will undoubtedly encounter significant milestones along the way. Such accomplishments are worth a pause for celebration! I remember reflecting on my son's focused reading instruction one year into taking the reins and realizing how far he had come in just twelve months. On that one-year anniversary, my struggling student shuffled through our deck of phonogram cards with ease, a task that had often felt wrought with uncertainty. As I paused to watch him and take in the blessing of progress, I was overwhelmed with gratitude and joy—a joy that propelled me into the following year with determination and purpose. Celebrating such milestones not only honors a job well done; it points to the Giver of good gifts, reorients our sights with fresh direction, and injects energy into routine instruction like a shot of endorphins on a long run.

Milestones of achievement don't just motivate parents and teachers, however. Celebrating long-term progress with your student in a tangible way offers him the chance to notice his own goals becoming reality. In our reading program, we celebrate the end of each reading level with a significant reward. These levels have taken us six to twelve months to complete, demanding sustained effort and productivity from the student. We've celebrated these milestones by filling out an official certificate, purchasing a longed-after toy, having dinner at a special restaurant, or purchasing a favorite team jersey—all gifts that depart from our normal mode of operation, thus emphasizing the significance of the accomplishment.

We also don't celebrate such milestones in isolation! One of the great joys of recognizing long-term achievement for struggling students is sharing that joy with others who have labored alongside them and supported their efforts. Classroom peers, other teachers, family members, and friends gain something incredibly valuable from this experience: they grow in understanding and, hopefully, in character as they witness uncommon determination, learn the value of patient help, and see Christian love in action. I have long argued that struggling students are not the only ones receiving benefits from the efforts of reading remediation and support for students with special needs.[4] Many, many times, parents, teachers, and friends find themselves sharpened and shaped by those we purportedly serve.

An Attitude of Optimism

This fall my child brought home a lengthy Scripture passage to be memorized over a period of several weeks. Even with a longer-than-normal timeframe for completion, the text before us left me with wide eyes and a furrowed brow: *Was this even attainable*? A generic outside evaluation seeking to match aptitude and ability might suggest my child should not attempt such a goal. But I am no outsider—and neither is my son.

After a discussion with my husband, we decided to ask our child directly how he felt about reading and memorizing the text, and then reciting this passage in front of his class, as the other students would do. I half-expected performance anxiety to derail this particular mission. However, my child's response indicated a view of struggle that has been honed through long walks in the trenches: "Yes, I want to do it. If I need help, I'm sure somebody will help me." I stood in awe—again. Here was a child who has *not* "gone it alone" for the past several years, floundering in a sea of struggle, bobbing up for gasps of air between waves of difficulty. Here was a child who has been given shoulders to

4. See Sara Osborne, "Moving Forward: Classically Educating Children with Special Needs," *The Classical Thistle*, September 11, 2018, https://theclassicalthis tle.com/2018/09/11/moving-forward-classically-educating-children-with-special -needs/.

lean on, hands to hold, and—at times—arms to carry him through the obstacles of academic life. These are not my shoulders, arms, and hands alone; a community of teachers, cheerleaders, supporters, and friends has helped give my son the courage to have a positive attitude despite the difficulty of a task. Such a cloud of witnesses is truly a powerful gift[5] and has drastic implications for cultivating an attitude of optimism that will serve students well in the long-range endeavor of learning to read.

Mind over Matter

While the old adage "attitude determines aptitude" may be cliché, its overuse stems from an undeniable truth: attitude makes a difference in outcome. We dare not downplay the role of attitude in moving struggling students towards reading fluency. Since human beings, by nature, do not pursue discouragement and difficulty, it stands to reason that struggling students would not exhibit an attitude of optimism and interest in a task that is fraught with (often severe) challenges for them—unless we help. In addition to incremental rewards for achievement, numerous strategies exist for promoting an attitude of teachability, interest, and eagerness in struggling readers.

As parents and teachers, we endeavor to promote a positive attitude toward learning and strive to compel our students' interest in reading remediation. To do this, we need to evaluate and consider: (1) how engaging our curriculum and practice are, (2) the clarity of our message that student identity is not bound up in performance, and (3) whether or not we are suggesting attainable goals that will build student confidence. Addressing these three components of attitude building will significantly impact a struggling student's productivity. Conversely,

5. See Hebrews 12:1, (ESV).

failure to consider them may hinder students from crossing the finish line of reading fluency and enjoying the fruits of the reading life.

Don't Forget to Have Fun

Recognizing the value of enjoyment in learning serves the overall educational endeavor. While parents and teachers rightly consider philosophy and method when considering how best to approach reading training, your struggling reader isn't likely to resonate with your research and inquiry. For your student, engaging texts and skill-building activities are the vehicles that will motivate and carry him past the mileposts on his way to the finish line. It's worth asking: *Is your reader having any fun?*

An acknowledgment that not every exercise will be fun is not the same as believing that none of them can be. As parents and teachers of students who are often leery of the reading process already, we can't afford to miss the difference. Sure, there will be days when we simply must read through an uninspiring list of practice words highlighting a particular phonogram, but that does not necessitate a prescription for all learning to take place via practice sheet. Looking for ways to make learning fun will help sustain student (and parent!) motivation.

If you are teaching your student yourself, hopefully you've chosen a curriculum with engaging texts and activities. This characteristic is one of the many reasons we chose to use the All About Reading curriculum: the text offers dimensional stories, enjoyable activities, and creative games for review. We've laughed at wily animal tales and empathized with stories of sibling squabbles. We've swatted words with a fly swatter (kids love the tactile satisfaction), giggled over intentionally humorous word mismatches, selected paper fruits for a gourmet smoothie, organized monster types, and zoomed race cars across phonogram tracks (I've even had a recent request to drive a remote-control car across ALL of our learned phonograms to date!). Such activities don't appear in every reading lesson, but they occur often enough that we've kept pace with our curriculum—and stayed motivated—for years.

In addition to the lessons and activities in our reading curriculum, we also look for other ways to make practicing reading—and visual skills in general—fun. Talking in silly voices, involving the family pet or stuffed animal, collecting books and magazines on a favorite topic, or sharing a video of reading practice with a friend can make reading tasks more enjoyable. Of course, what constitutes enjoyment will vary across personality and age. Still, options abound for board games, electronic games, puzzle books, crafts, and other fun activities that reinforce critical reading skills. Incorporating joy into your reading program is not only essential for motivation; it also reminds your student that her side of the experience is worth considering.

Worth More Than Words

When we teach and encourage in a way that pursues the joy of our students, we remind them that their value is not determined by their output; they are far more valuable to us than the phonograms they've acquired, the number of words they can decode, or the speed at which they can read. As a steady, committed presence on good reading days and bad ones, parents and teachers have the opportunity to motivate struggling students by reminding them that their identity is not determined by performance.

Over years of reading instruction, we've had our share of bad days. I was reminded one particularly hard day of how my reaction to struggle shapes my child's view of himself. My son was limping through a lesson, frustrated at himself and clearly grasping for motivation to continue on. I don't remember the cause of the irritability—perhaps a misunderstanding with a friend or a run-in on the playground at recess—but I can still see his concerned face in my mind, searching for reassurance amidst his poor performance. Whatever the catalyst for the frustration, something was interfering with his ability to access the information he needed for reading, and he quickly grew discouraged.

In such moments, it's easy for parents and teachers to process discouragement as despair, especially early on! However, after months and years with days like this, I've learned that panic never serves either of us well. In fact, one of the most compassionate ways I can serve my student is to show him visibly that I am not shocked by struggle, I am not going anywhere, and I am committed to weathering these storms together. While I may be battling my own feelings on the inside, I pray for strength to show my child that I am not in a hurry; I am with him for the long run. Not only does a teacher's quiet, stalwart confidence empower a struggling learner, but it also demonstrates unconditional love. Your assuring presence shapes how your student sees his value, even on bad days. In a world where struggling readers will always feel the pressure of underperformance, such students need constant reminders that their value is found not in their output—but in the fact that they are loved. What a privilege it is to be the speaker of such truth!

Make It Attainable

Experience teaches us that feelings of failure tend to grow exponentially. Have you ever sacrificed a roll of quarters to the claw machine in a restaurant lobby or arcade? Children across the nation can be seen begging parents for *just one more chance* at retrieving a giant neon teddy bear, propelled on by the fact that the claw *nearly got it* the last time. Most anyone with claw machine experience recognizes the futility of attempting to guide the claw to a choice stuffed animal—surely the chances are one in a thousand at best! We (rightly) grow reluctant to keep throwing valuable money or effort at tasks that appear futile. Maybe a poor soul without any previous claw machine experience will give it a go once or twice, but soon failure steals his motivation, and the endeavor comes to an end.

So it goes with learning. Students will not make progress if they aren't presented with *any* difficulty—with new concepts necessary for mastery of a particular skill. Yet neither will they move forward if the task is unbearably arduous and achievement is nowhere to be found. Our task as parents and teachers is to *keep learning attainable.* One linguistic expert hypothesized that effective language acquisition results from teaching to the next level—the next rung on the ladder—beyond the content our students have already mastered: "The language that learners are exposed to should be just far enough beyond their current competence that they can understand most of it but still be challenged to make progress."[6] That means we don't stay where we are, but we don't place unrealistic expectations on our students either.

Learning to decode a text requires careful, systematic skill building. While some students can leap intuitively at intervals across the explicit teaching of certain reading rules, struggling readers need incremental instruction that moves them ever closer to reading fluency. Hopping and skipping haphazardly from one phonics lesson or decoding rule to another without an organized trajectory will leave your reader feeling unnecessarily discouraged. We've noticed similar negative results when practice texts accompanying a reading curriculum include language far beyond what the student should be able to decipher.[7] Struggling learners are motivated to reach for new reading

6. This is the basis of Stephen Krashen's *Input Hypothesis.* See H. Douglas Brown, *Principles of Language Learning and Teaching* (New York: Longman, 2000), 278.

7. This isn't an argument against ever exposing your reader to sophisticated language (in fact, exposing struggling readers to unfamiliar language through read-alouds and audiobooks is critical), but rather an observation that students need prac-

skills when they sense that the goal is attainable. Following a program that adds one building block at a time to the foundation your student is already building will motivate him to keep going. Do continue to read aloud to your student above his or her grade level, but provide practice texts that match your child's decoding knowledge. A steady pattern of such instruction builds motivation, stamina, and trust.

Significance of Community

Motivation doesn't just spring from shaping a reader's activities and attitude; it also flows from a connection to others. A supportive community significantly impacts motivation for any challenging endeavor. Difficulty leaves us feeling defeated—and often lonely—if we feel that no one else shares our experience. This is true for struggling learners *and* those who love and serve them. Children without committed parents, teachers, and friends who will support them lose a valuable asset in the fight for motivation and progress. And parents and teachers who feel like they are shouldering the burden alone are likely to crumble under the resulting weight of isolation.

Family members, friends, teachers, doctors, and therapists have played a critical role as motivators in our reading training. My son's teachers—past and present—follow his progress (I texted a photo displaying a certificate of completion for AAR Level 3 to teachers three grades back!). We share milestones and successes with family and friends. My child's classmates even share in the joy of his accomplishments. At times, such support looks like cheers, hugs, and high-fives. Last year, it took the form of one student patiently helping my son read a book he had written for a school contest out loud to the class.

---

tice texts that match the skills they are learning—or hover just above it—in order to increase motivation for reading.

As parents and teachers, we seem less apt to acknowledge the motivating effect community has on *us* just as it does our struggling learners, but adults are not immune from the discouragement of isolation. I remember with clarity the relief of shared understanding that washed over me during our first vision consultation with Dr. Pierce. I can't recall a single visit after that (and there have been many) in which he hasn't left me with the simple kindness, "Hang in there; you're a good mom." I also vividly remember sitting in a wooden classroom chair with my child's teachers surrounding me, praying through tears for wisdom, creative insight, and perseverance as we sought to tackle academic challenges. I think back on times I sobbed into my phone out of frustration and despair, only to hear the gentle words of a parent telling me I was doing something hard but worthwhile. My husband has been a constant support, working alongside me towards the growth of all our children, and the kids themselves are a constant reminder of the worth of education. My home team offers motivation when I'm tempted to feel alone.

Two (or Three?) Are Better Than One

I rarely run alone these days; I log most of my weekly mileage with my husband, and often with one of our German Shorthaired Pointers ranging out in front. Still, there is a contagious energy when we enter a race full of hundreds of like-minded athletes. We smile and nod in camaraderie to each runner we pass. We strike up conversations with those running a similar pace and share battle stories about the struggle of *that one killer hill*. We cheer in unison as the few phenoms jockeying for first place double-back on the trail just minutes after the rest of us have ascended the first mountaintop. Somehow their success isn't threatening—it only seems to stoke the palpable zeal extending from one runner to another. The energy is intoxicating; together, we're all an integral part of the race.

If you feel like you're running your race alone, allow me to encourage you to pursue community with like-minded teachers, parents, and friends. Don't underestimate the significance of your own motivation in training your struggling reader. You are pouring time, energy, emotion, and effort into a long but worthy endeavor, one that is often just plain hard. Finding others who understand both the burden and the joy can be transformational. It's difficult to run a marathon in isolation. Perhaps it can be done—but not without a cost.

CH. 5 "NOTES FROM THE TRAINER": A FEW QUESTIONS & ANSWERS FROM DR. DAVID PIERCE, OD

How have you seen attitude affect reading remediation or vision therapy?

Attitude enables achievement. Give me a client who is motivated and hopeful, and I will show you progress! I once had a sixteen-year-old client whose parents dragged him into my office. They wanted me to turn him into a reader. When I asked the young man if he wanted to learn to read, he said, "Not really." At the parents' request, I showed him some tools, offered affirmation that the young man had the ability to do what was needed, and told him I hoped he would come back and find me when he was ready. Some time passed, and that young man eventually did come back to my office. He had enough motivation to sway his attitude, and he committed himself to the work. His attitude made all the difference in his progress toward becoming the kind of reader he wanted to be.

I can recall another set of parents who brought their child in for an evaluation, hoping that I could help him with reading. The father watched me suspiciously as I did some tests with their child. When I asked the father if he had any questions about what I was doing, he offered a curt "No," without any further response. When the family left, the father seemed entirely uninterested in anything I had tried to say. When I saw the child again for an evaluation, the father came bounding in, ready to receive new tools to help his child. His wife even commented on how he had started doing homework with their son, a sight that had not occurred prior to their son's perceptual therapy at our clinic. The father himself disclosed what had changed: he simply hadn't believed anything could help his son. When his son began to show signs of progress, the father's attitude progressed in tandem. Two engaged parents now helped their son acquire new visual skills, and success followed their efforts.

Once a parent understands how their child thinks, and realizes there are strategies to help him, it's a game changer. They will still get frustrated at times, but their attitude—and often their child's attitude—changes from desperation and defeat to *hope*. This is especially true when parents begin to understand the difference between the way they think and how their child thinks.

What has helped motivate your most successful clients?

My most successful clients have been the ones who came in with no confidence and then they gained confidence. Many clients come to me as a "last stop" after trying numerous other interventions. They come in feeling the weight of failure. Sometimes they're embarrassed, sometimes they've been labeled and isolated. When they encounter their first taste of success, a new confidence blooms—and every subsequent success causes them to crave more. For such clients, once they realized they could read—once they experienced success—there was no stopping them. Their zeal carried them forward toward the finish line.

How important is community for struggling readers and their parents?

A solid support system significantly affects the success of my clients. It's important to consider primary influencers (mom/dad/teacher), secondary influencers (grandparents, a coach), and tertiary influencers (friends). Because we tend to model our lives after those closest to us, primary influencers have a substantial impact on who a child becomes. Accordingly, it's critical for primary influencers to get on the same page in order to reach the child. If they are expecting a child with opposite tendencies to be just like them, their pressure on the child may cause him to flounder. Their efforts at intervention will likely fail. On the other hand, if they endeavor to learn how to best help this child they love, it can bear fruit exponentially.

A true story illustrates this point: A client's mother was frustrated at his inability to read. She couldn't understand how this child could be "so unlike her." She poured out her disdain to me with an animated face and flailing gestures while her son sat quietly in his father's lap. Months later, they returned to my office somewhat transformed. The child's mother had realized how significantly her emotional responses had impacted her relationship with her son (and, as a result, his reading progress) and had made a conscious effort to approach him with patience and restraint. The beautiful result was a stronger mother-son relationship, a motivated child, and the successful removal of roadblocks to reading. Reading success is often just as much about what we learn to do differently as parents as it is about creating a new system for the child. Understanding that truth can be transformative for families of struggling students.

Injury Prevention & Treatment

On mile eighteen of twenty down a familiar country road, my body instinctively slammed on the brakes at a piercing pain in my right knee. With just a few miles left in my longest training run to date, I struggled to shake off the pain and keep going, but my efforts proved futile. I simply wasn't able to keep running, and no amount of denial, regret, anger, or determination would move me closer to my goal. Despite weeks and months of training, I was instantly sidelined, and my spirits took an immediate downturn. I had no choice but to saunter back home, acknowledging my injury.

Research suggests that more than 50 percent of runners are injured annually[1]—a hefty statistic for such a healthy pursuit. These injuries vary in origin and manifestation, of course, but most stem from issues related to overuse. Over time, repeated stress on bones, muscles, and ligaments can lead to irritation, inflammation, and even tears or fractures. Such problems can sideline runners for days, weeks, or even months, depending on the severity of the injury. These setbacks carry both physical and emotional tolls; the healing process is often as much

---

1. "Running Injuries," Yale Medicine, accessed October 8, 2022, https://www.yalemedicine.org/conditions/running-injury.

a mental game as a physical one. Still, a runner's prognosis for recovery is often positive when he or she follows through with appropriate amounts of rest, strengthening exercises, cross-training, and a good return-to-running program.

My own running life supports current injury statistics. During my years on the road and on the trail, I've endured multiple stress fractures, numerous bouts of tendinitis, iliotibial band syndrome, and sacroiliac joint dysfunction. At times, one injury has been directly followed by another, revealing my body's attempt to compensate for weakness in one area by unduly taxing a different area—adding a double dose of frustration. Some injuries have healed quickly, while others tested my commitment and resolve for months on end. None of them were welcome, and all required determination to overcome.

Reading Obstacles

While you may not place reading in the same category as physical exercise, struggling readers endure "injuries" and setbacks consistent with other challenging long-range tasks. Undue academic or emotional stress, neglecting the effects of sickness or eye strain, or even experiencing a common cold can sideline a reader for days, causing mental frustration and emotional despondency. Often, one obstacle is closely followed by another, doubly disheartening parent, teacher, and child. The reality is that for students with heightened needs for reading remediation, any slight hindrance can become a major factor in reading performance and growth. We are whole people, and stresses in any area of life can create obstacles for reading instruction.

During the early months of the COVID-19 pandemic, most budding readers encountered numerous obstacles to their learning routines. While some children—and their family members—were beset with illness, others woke up to new ways of doing key tasks nearly every day, removing feelings of safety and calm built on scaffolds of routine. In-person instruction ceased at schools worldwide, and households were filled with commotion and noise. The best teachers and parents were thrown into new territory, striving to keep all kinds of students moving forward.

In the winter of 2020, COVID finally found its way to our house. Despite our best mitigation efforts, we fell ill—two by two, like animals boarding the ark! Thankfully, our symptoms were mild, and no one required serious medical care. That does not mean, however, that we remained symptom-free. Sore throats and sneezes quickly turned into runny noses, which turned into cough and fatigue and feelings of general misery that all cold-like illness seems to bring. Tiredness and cognitive fog persisted, affecting memory, productivity, and clarity of thought. The youngest among us weren't immune to these symptoms; two of our children struggled to find normalcy for days after being cleared to return to school. And once their physical health was restored, they felt emotionally overwhelmed by the pressure of missed lessons and mounting homework.

It should come as no surprise, then, that while reading lessons with my son resumed, they were far from fruitful. We marched dutifully onward in our study and practice, but we failed to make notable progress. Some days I was tempted to wonder if I was doing more damage than good. Earlier in this reading journey, I would have resorted to despair, wondering if we would ever push through what felt like a never-ending valley. *But we had walked in valleys before, and we hadn't stayed there forever.* Remembering is such good medicine for the soul!

While our family had not endured pandemic-style illness before, we had certainly encountered "off days"—or weeks—in which we made little to no progress. Head colds and stuffy noses leave the most committed students wanting to crawl into bed with cozy blankets and forget about the world. Emotional stresses—from a dispute with friends at the playground to the death of a pet or loved one—drain struggling students of their ability to focus and perform. A broken bone or bad case of poison ivy can be so distracting that a child can think of little else. Even excitement over an upcoming party or vacation can cause distraction and slow productivity. Parents and teachers know well that every child has a different level of sensitivity to stress, whether it be physical or emotional. Over time, careful watching and listening will help you determine when to push and when to pause.

Diagnosis, Treatment, & Recovery

With observation and experience, you can become more adept at noticing how outside stressors affect your student's reading progress. Note physical symptoms (squinting, rubbing, eye redness, eye drifting, sniffling, coughing) as well as emotional ones (visible anger or frustration, preoccupation with discussing bothersome events or experiences, sadness, despondency). Strive to pay attention to the other relationships affecting your student's days—friendships, teachers, and siblings—and other tasks vying for his time—projects at school, upcoming tests, new concepts being learned, or an exciting field trip. Such assessments provide valuable clues to help determine when to apply appropriate pressure and when to give space for rest, reflection, and recuperation.

Check Your Pace

Of course, refusing to deviate from planned instruction and throwing in the towel are not the only two options for parents and teachers who encounter frazzled readers! When injury, illness, or other obstacles appear, I often opt to modify our plans to keep us moving forward without the kind of pressure that will exacerbate stress. Sometimes, this simply means *slowing down*. Just as it does for a runner seeking to finish a race with a piercing side cramp, slowing down the pace of instruction and practice can provide a reduction in pressure and the opportunity to regain momentum that your struggling reader needs. Remember, training a struggling reader is a long-range endeavor! The goal is not necessarily to maintain pace with your child's peers; instead, a focus on steady, productive movement toward the finish line will best direct your efforts. A focus on someone else's pace may prolong sickness or lead to emotional explosions that serve neither the student nor his instructor. Monitor your student's response to obstacles and adapt accordingly.

Sometimes simply slowing the pace of instruction isn't an adequate strategy for combatting the stress a student is experiencing. In such cases, it may be appropriate to stop the lesson altogether, choosing instead to use that time for rest or calming activities: take a short walk, pet the family dog, listen to soothing music, or drink a warm beverage. During the rare occasions when we abandon a lesson completely, I've found that the most important messages for me to communicate to my struggling learner are (1) resting isn't the same as quitting, (2) I have not now become convinced that this endeavor is futile, and (3) we will continue moving forward when and how it is appropriate. He needs to know that I am with him; I'm not going anywhere, and when he is ready, we will move forward side by side. The vast majority of the time, my determined optimism meets him like a rescue rope; he can hold on to it and pull himself out of despair.

Modifying Instruction

Opportunities abound for modifying instruction on stressful days. Playing a review game, reading books on a favorite topic (even those well beneath your student's reading level—*some* reading is better than *no* reading!), increasing fluency with texts that your student has already read (less intimidating/tiring), or taking turns reading sections of a particular passage can motivate a student who isn't in a place to digest new information or practice new concepts. (See more on motivation in chapter 5). If your child is simply having an "off day," it shouldn't be difficult to pick back up where you left off. When the obstacle you've encountered lasts several days or more, consider setting benchmarks to help facilitate your return-to-reading plan—just like a sidelined runner planning her comeback. If your child is ill, this might include suggestions and prescriptions from medical professionals. If your child has endured emotional trauma, consider recommendations from a professional counselor when constructing your plan. Regardless of the members of your planning team, thinking past the "injury" will serve both teacher and student; an anticipated route back to your normal training routine communicates both an acknowledgment that treatment is necessary for healing and that there must be an incremental, measured path back toward reading progress.

Preventing Setbacks Before They Start

Some obstacles to reading training simply cannot be helped. Just like the most elite runners, if a child is sick, his body will not perform at its highest capability. If he is worried about a relational issue or academic problem, his mind will be distracted. If he is generally exhausted, he will not demonstrate his best skills. However, there are steps we can take to avoid illness, distraction, and burnout in the first place.

A Healthy Outlook

Perhaps it goes without saying that a student's overall physical health is integral to his reading success, but do you consider health and nutrition to be a critical component of your child's reading training? Research suggests that we ought to take this more seriously. Regular exercise has lasting impacts on brain development and health, affecting cognitive function, which propels your reader's progress. According to researchers, the effects of exercise on learning and memory are both direct and indirect: "The benefits from exercise come directly from its ability to reduce insulin resistance, reduce inflammation, and stimulate the release of growth factors—chemicals in the brain that affect the health of brain cells, the growth of new blood vessels in the brain, and even the abundance and survival of new brain cells. Indirectly, exercise improves mood and sleep, and reduces stress and anxiety. Problems in these areas frequently cause cognitive impairment."[2] Since struggling readers often face both cognitive challenges and emotional stressors, including exercise in any long-term training plan directly lines up with current research. Not only will your child's mind be affected, but his whole body will be strengthened to fight illness and injury!

The Importance of Diet

In addition to exercise, good nutrition helps build a strong body and immune system responsible for warding off illness. Research demonstrates the impact of diet on cognitive function, something parents and teachers of struggling readers should take seriously.[3] Studies show that a healthy diet may merit particular significance for students with learning challenges. For example, omega-3 fatty acids have demon-

---

2. Heidi Godman, "Regular Exercise Changes the Brain to Improve Memory, Thinking Skills," Harvard Health Publishing, Harvard Medical School, April 9, 2014, https://www.health.harvard.edu/blog/regular-exercise-changes-brain-improve-mem ory-thinking-skills-201404097110.

3. Fernando Gómez-Pinilla, "Brain Foods: The Effects of Nutrients on Brain Functioning," National Library of Medicine, National Center for Biotechnology Information, accessed October 8, 2022, https://www.ncbi.nlm.nih.gov/pmc/articles /PMC2805706/.

strated effects on the cognitive processes of learning and memory; deficits in this nutrient have even been associated with dyslexia.[4] Folate and vitamin E have also demonstrated positive effects on healthy cognition. Conversely, "studies indicate that diets with high contents of *trans* and saturated fats adversely affect cognition."[5] While most parents and teachers acknowledge that "junk food" may lead to obesity or poor dental health, many are unaware of the high stakes that a poor diet has for struggling learners in particular. Findings from studies on the effects of "junk food" suggest that "the diet had a direct effect on neurons. . . .This diet elevated the neurological burden that was associated with experimental brain injury, as evidenced by worse performance in learning tasks."[6] In an already difficult endeavor, poor nutrition only compounds the struggle for training readers. Evaluating, improving, and/or supplementing your child's diet gives him the best nutritional resources possible for the task of reading remediation.

An Interest in Intake

A student's diet does not merely consist of food, however; his daily intake includes books, music, movies, lectures, and other forms of media. He consumes both information and entertainment, for information and for pleasure. Certainly, all of this consumption affects a child (a topic worth considering at length in a separate book!),[7] but as parents and teachers focused on helping struggling readers, we should be acutely aware of their textual intake. For such students, a healthy diet of literature is nearly as important as a colorful plate of nutritious food!

4. Ibid.
5. Ibid.
6. Ibid.
7. For an excellent discussion of the effects of media consumption, see Brett McCracken's book *The Wisdom Pyramid* (Wheaton: Crossway, 2021).

We assess the value of books based on a variety of criteria: interesting stories, well-crafted characters, truthful information, excellent artwork, relevant content, or readable font, to name a few. Bookshops and libraries are full of wonderful children's literature—but finding it may require some digging. Unfortunately, an overemphasis on attraction and entertainment has left the children's section of most libraries anemic. Children plead for the latest *Lego: Ninjago* or *Pokémon* reader because they recognize familiar titles and characters, but the books themselves leave something to be desired. The stories are flat, the characters lack depth, and the word choice and descriptive language found in the best of children's literature are all but absent. What was meant for a colorful, fast-paced, animated viewing has been transposed onto paper—and it isn't as good in print.

So, what is a reading instructor to do? How do we encourage fledgling readers without filling our bookshelves with Disney princess stories and transcribed *Teenage Mutant Ninja Turtles* episodes? Several strategies can help parents and teachers navigate the mass of literary options: (1) familiarize yourself with titles of classic children's literature, (2) consult excellent book lists from trusted sources,[8] and (3) skim or scan shorter books for readable font,[9] character depth, storyline, and overall beauty. You may even note a preferred publisher or a par-

---

8. For help finding good children's literature, consider beginning with one of the following online resources: Sarah Mackenzie's Read-Aloud Revival (www.readaloudrevival.com), The Fordham Institute's "Kindergarten Canon" (https://fordhaminstitute.org/national/commentary/kindergarten-canon-100-best-childrens-books), or The Gospel Coalition's "Complete Classical Christian School Reading List for Grades 1–8" (https://www.thegospelcoalition.org/blogs/justin-taylor/a-complete-classical-christian-school-reading-list-grades-1-8/).

9. Font size and clarity can make a significant difference in readability for students with visual processing problems. We've found the readers from Bellwether Media to be helpful in this respect. The lower-level readers contain large, easy-to-read font, with smaller text size and more words per page in subsequent levels.

ticular series that meets your requirements. The point is that you are monitoring your student's intake and encouraging healthy habits.

All learners—young and old—should seek to read widely. There is surely a place for entertainment and relaxation alongside character development and intellectual growth. Encouraging a child to love good literature doesn't mean that he should never set eyes on a printed episode of *PAW Patrol*; it simply means we should make an effort to not let his entire diet of literature be comprised of such books. Like most healthy habits, nutritious intake should be the norm, and the occasional "junk" should be the exception. In a world of advertisements and marketing, our children will have plenty of reasons to ask for the "junk." It's up to us to provide compelling reasons for them to choose something else.[10]

The Dangers of Digital Media?

Perhaps even more concerning than the allure of chintzy children's literature is the effect of digital media on the reading brain. Author and neuroscientist Maryann Wolf's book *Reader Come Home: The Reading Brain in the Digital World* explores and imagines the impact of technology on a child's reading training. Wolf argues that the explosive exposure of children to digital media is resulting in dramatic losses of attention and memory—two necessary components for reading acquisition. Such attention deficits stem from chronic stimulation:

> In the development of cognition . . . children learn to focus their attention with ever more concentration and duration from in-

10. See also Sara Osborne, "Engaging Young Readers: Building a Healthy Diet of Good Books," *The Classical Thistle*, September 27, 2018, https://theclassicalthistle.com/2018/09/27/engaging-young-readers-building-a-healthy-diet-of-good-books/.

fancy through adolescence. Learning to concentrate is an essential but ever more difficult challenge in a culture where distraction is omnipresent. Young adults may learn to be less affected when moving from one stimulus to another because they have more fully formed inhibitory systems that, at least in principle, provide the option of overriding continuous distraction. Not so with younger children, whose systems and other executive planning functions in their frontal cortex need a long time to develop. Attention, in the very young, is up for grabs.[11]

In addition to affecting how well a child attends to the task of reading, digital media also poses threats to memory. Working memory is particularly important in the pursuit of literacy, and research suggests that attention-stealing technology may have serious effects on memory, and thus reading comprehension.[12] Wolf postulates:

> If changes in working memory begin to occur, changes in long-term memory would also be predicted. If both are changed, we would predict downstream effects on children's building of their background knowledge. The latter, in turn, would impact the development and deployment of multiple deep-reading skills in the formative period of the young reading circuit.[13]

Numerous case studies testify to the benefits of modern technology in accommodating learners of all types and creating avenues for reading (audiobooks, e-readers, assistive software) that were once

11. Maryann Wolf, *Reader Come Home: The Reading Brain in a Digital World*, (New York: HarperCollins, 2018), 108.
12. Ibid., 116.
13. Ibid., 115.

only imagined. However, a wise reading instructor will consider Wolf's warning: these benefits may come at a cost. Evaluating the volume and type of digital media your student consumes, considering its effects, and limiting intake accordingly will help you avoid the obstacles of reduced attention and lower working memory for your reader-in-training.

The Critical Role of Rest

Parents and teachers who have identified a struggling reader rightly want to *do something* about it. We've identified a problem and long to solve it—surely that requires action! Indeed, it does, but—perhaps counterintuitively—it also requires understanding the importance of rest. Any parent who has prodded children from summer to school-year scheduling knows how sleep patterns affect mood, motivation, and performance. The long, lazy days and late nights of summer leave children ill-prepared for the mental focus and physical stamina they need during the school year. This change in demand requires a change in routine—which often results in earlier bedtimes and planned times to recharge. I daresay this phenomenon is true for most of us—but its impact on struggling readers is extraordinary.

Research studies aren't necessary to prove the increased cognitive demand on struggling readers (although they support it well).[14] I can see it with my own eyes. Facial expression, posture, and other body language reveal what I already know to be true: reading lessons are hard

14. For example, low visual-information processing speed has been linked to increased student fatigue in elementary and junior high school students. See Kei Mizuno et al., "Low Visual-Information Processing Speed and Attention Are Predictors of Fatigue in Elementary and Junior High School Students," National Library of Medicine, National Center for Biotechnology Information, Accessed October 11, 2022, https://www.ncbi.nlm.nih.gov/pmc/articles/PMC3126715/.

work for a child with learning challenges. Reading instruction, reading as a component of regular academic life, and the increase in homework that often accompanies slow or below-level reading yields fatigue that cannot be ignored. Parents and teachers must acknowledge the very real need for such students to *rest* if progress is to be attained.

Rest comes in a variety of forms, and numerous strategies exist for building it into a routine for reading training. The most obvious form of rest is sleep—a significant contributor to cognitive ability and growth[15]—but it's not the only factor to consider. Eliminating distractions in a learning environment, reducing visual clutter (particularly on reading material, handouts, and assignments), and providing a clear set of expectations for a child's day or week also promote rest for a reader-in-training. Helping students broaden their language stores through audiobooks, theater performances, and concerts provides an opportunity to take in vocabulary and story in a less pressured setting. Utilizing creative practice activities can offer a restful mental break from more structured lessons.

In *Leisure: The Basis of Culture*, Joseph Pieper suggests that the very essence of education should involve a sense of rest. In fact, we get the English word "school" from the Latin *scola* or Greek *skole*, meaning "leisure." However, Pieper is quick to point out that our contemporary use of this word may be too constricting:

> Leisure, it must be clearly understood, is a mental and spiritual attitude—it is not simply the result of external factors, it is not the

---

15. Deborah Kotz, "Children Who Lack Sleep May Experience Detrimental Impact on Brain and Cognitive Development That Persists Over Time, UM School of Medicine Study Finds," July 29, 2022, https://www.medschool.umaryland.edu/news/2022/Children-Who-Lack-Sleep-May-Experience-Detrimental-Impact-on-Brain-and-Cognitive-Development-That-Persists-Over-Time-UM-School-of-Medicine-Study-Finds.htm.

inevitable result of spare time, a holiday, a weekend or a vacation. It is, in the first place, an attitude of mind, a condition of the soul.[16]

A student whose parent or teacher models such a posture towards learning has a remarkable advantage: not only will his education consist of more than a utilitarian quest, but he will find an encouraging peace in the midst of a challenging endeavor.

In our family's own pursuit of rest, I've become acutely aware of the role *I* play in creating a peaceful learning environment. When I am harried, impatient, and distracted, my child absorbs that stress. *My* frustration and rush lead *him* to bristle and worry; conversely, my focus and calm call him to attentiveness and growth. The root of this restlessness is usually a type of unbelief—a temporary lapse into clamoring for control over my schedule, my child, or the learning process itself instead of trusting the God of time and humanity. Unsurprisingly, this is the very opposite of *leisure* according to Pieper:

> Leisure is not the attitude of mind of those who actively intervene, but of those who are open to everything; not of those who grab and grab hold, but of those who leave the reins loose and who are free and easy themselves—almost like a man falling asleep, for one can only fall asleep by "letting oneself go."[17]

Some days I act my way into promoting such peace. I don't think of this as hypocrisy, but rather as an act of love—love for my child, which motivates the fight against the temptation to overreact to claims on my

---

16. Joseph Pieper, *Leisure: The Basis of Culture* (San Fransisco: Ignatius Press, 2009), 19.

17. Pieper, *Leisure*, 47.

time and energy or his momentary struggle. And, in God's good providence, loving another person ends up not only affecting him—but also changing me for the better. Pursuing a life of *scholé* serves us both.

Cross-Training Through Creative Skill Practice

When athletes experience illness or injury that sidelines their training, they often turn to cross-training—using another exercise to maintain or even increase overall strength and stamina. However, cross-training also serves as an effective tool for injury *prevention*. For athletes whose bodies encounter repeated stress to the same bones, muscles, and ligaments with every run, cross-training offers an opportunity to enhance fitness and prevent injury before it starts.

Strengthening "overall fitness" through creative skill building offers the same boost to struggling readers. Students need a specific set of reading skills in order to read well, but learning to read also requires the more global skills of attentiveness, observation, problem-solving, physical stamina, the ability to follow instructions, and eventual independence. Reading curricula and texts are certainly not the only tools for building such skills!

Early on in our journey with visual processing disorder and reading challenges, our optometrist-friend suggested that our son would learn to leverage his strengths to compensate for his weaknesses. Dr. Pierce's message was both literal and figurative: perhaps without even thinking about it, our son would learn unconventional ways of processing visual information in order to complete necessary tasks, but he would also find the motivation to overcome weaknesses by identifying and enjoying activities he loves. For some time, such activities remained elusive. With lesser visual skills, any sport involving visual-motor coordination posed difficulty. Enjoyment—not to mention success—in most school subjects was largely dependent on reading ability and visual processing skills. Most music instructors want a child to have basic reading proficiency before beginning to learn an instrument. Building and design also require strong visual-spatial skills. Ever observing and mindful of the high stakes of building both skill and confidence, we watched and waited to find something our son really *loved* doing.

The answer came in the form of a puppy. One sunny Saturday in February, my husband loaded our van and headed to Kansas to pick up the dog who would become "Osborne's Regis Pippa's Song." Our son was immediately smitten. He fed, watered, and snuggled this little German Shorthaired Pointer with great care, and we watched with anticipation to see how she would grow. By late spring, both puppy and handler were ready to begin their training sessions. Mornings before school and evenings after dinner found my husband and son out in the backyard, repeating simple commands, time after time. As I watched from the kitchen window, I couldn't help but think of how these short training sessions were developing character and skill in my son; he was developing attentiveness, persistence, commitment, and perseverance with every step. He learned to listen to instruction and follow multi-step directions. He discovered how to be assertive and speak with a confident voice. He began to sense the importance of timing. He failed, and he learned from his mistakes. And all of these gains were made possible because of a singular passion for working dogs.

Over the past two years, we've watched our son's passion for pointing dogs affect numerous areas of his development. Like many active young boys, he doesn't immediately reach for a book to entertain himself, but he will read books about the German Shorthaired Pointer breed. Memory work is an arduous task for him, but he can list—in order—the various parts of a natural ability test for hunting dogs. Public speaking and independent work often induce anxiety for our son, but just months into training, he led his dog out into a field for the AKC Junior

Hunt Test with independence and confidence. Our son's vocabulary has broadened, and his understanding of the natural world has grown. He is figuring out how to leverage his strengths to compensate for his weaknesses. He is stronger and tougher; he has grown in myriad ways.

Finding a way for struggling students to plan for, execute, and achieve any goal can forge valuable character formation and skill development integral to reading training. Struggling learners often lack motivation and confidence, yet parents and teachers have the unique opportunity to promote these qualities if we will look for what sparks joy in the heart of each child. What does your child love? What does he talk about? What makes her glow? What brings him delight? Look for an ember you can fan into a flame. Identifying and encouraging a struggling reader's passions might serve him in ways you can't even imagine now, prompting plentiful growth and unspeakable joy.

Renewable Energy

More than two decades into my running life, the level and intensity of my running still waxes and wanes with the rhythms of my days. My responsibilities as wife, mother, teacher, and friend often mean shorter runs or more time off than I would like. Scheduled events and unscheduled sickness sometimes interrupt my best intentions to stay fit and keep my mileage up. Last fall, my husband and I spent four months training for a long-distance race, increasing our mileage with every consecutive week. After the race was over, we both vocalized a desire to not let our stamina slip away. Yet holiday events and travel combined with wintertime illness quickly derailed our determination, and we found ourselves back on the track in early February feeling like we had never run a lap before! We slogged through those foundation-building miles in silence, the chatty energy of our runs just months earlier eluding us.

Thankfully, feelings don't always indicate reality—and, in our case, that held to be true. In fact, research suggests that regular runners actually rebound from time off faster than non-runners, thanks to the phenomenon we call "muscle memory."[18] Our bodies are conditioned from years of running so that we actually return to previous levels of fitness faster—just one of the many benefits of the running life!

Long-term reading instruction yields similar results: years of repetition and practice have cultivated a "reading memory" for my child that helps him bounce back, even after bouts of sickness or scheduled time away from his regular reading lessons. Months of structured, systematic lessons enable this rebound. Time off can induce anxiety for both parents and their children. However, teachers and students need not fear the loss of all that has been gained when unavoidable interruptions invade the lesson schedule; over time, the runway to reentry will get shorter and shorter. Your child is blazing well-worn trails that aren't easily covered up. Consistency in the long haul will have its reward.

Ch. 6 "Notes from the Trainer": A Few Questions & Answers from Dr. David Pierce, OD

Have you seen evidence of rest, diet, and/or exercise affecting the success of visual skill building/reading remediation?

> Overall health does play a role in remedying visual issues. For example, I had a client with diabetes who was experiencing some severe visual impairment. The condition of his eyes was so severe that I couldn't help him until we dealt with the diabetic response.

18. J. C. Bruusgaard et al., "Myonuclei Acquired by Overload Exercise Precede Hypertrophy and Are Not Lost on Detraining," PNAS, National Academy of Science, August 16, 2010, https://www.pnas.org/doi/10.1073/pnas.0913935107.

After speaking to his primary care physician, I became aware that although this client was diabetic, he was drinking 2 two-liters of Dr. Pepper every day, choosing to ignore the obvious implications for his body—and especially for his eyes. An unwillingness to address his diet was prohibiting him from getting help with his visual system. This is an extreme example, but the principle is true for considering the role of healthy habits in general. Our bodies are comprised of individual parts that are integrated into functional systems. A failure to consider one part of that system often has a significant impact on its efficiency and success.

Do you see "injuries" (obstacles) stemming from too much screen time? Is this significant for struggling readers?

I differentiate between productive and addictive screen time. Children who spend hours on video games or social media will suffer negative consequences for their visual systems and attention spans. Kids who spend four hours reading on an electronic reading tablet show different results. The contrast and options for reading on a tablet (designed for reading) are not problematic, visually.

When I ask about screen time, I ask parents if it's a problem, an addiction. If a child plays hours of video games every day, his neurological function is being altered. His endorphins are heightened, and he won't make reading (or any academic) progress.

Dialogue makes the biggest difference here. Explaining to a child that he is irritable because he spent four hours on a video game helps him understand what's happening. It offers him agency over his actions and their consequences. Increased awareness and maturity over time helps enable a child to self-regulate and engage in learning. Of course, until that develops, the responsibility for instruction and intervention lies with parents.

In what ways have you seen creative skill building ("cross-training") lead to gains in visual skill/reading?

Exposing struggling readers to options for engaging activities is important. These are building moments that come with cognitive maturity. Having time to observe and process an activity or skill and then engage in it promotes confidence in struggling students. When you find those things that really motivate and build confidence, then something clicks and there is newfound independence and joy. This is success outside of reading and spelling that builds motivation and tenacity that is transferrable to other difficult tasks (like reading!). The child gains a positive mentality that affects everything else he does—a valuable asset for students with special needs.

Race Day: Crossing the Finish Line

I listened to his words with my eyes closed, relishing the echoes of fluid sound, whole words, rising and falling intonation. We were just at the office for a six-month progress exam, but at this point in our long run to reading, such moments feel tantamount to planting a flag on the moon: we have come far—and yet we're just beginning. The reading portion of the exam ended not long after it commenced, but for those sixty seconds, time stood still, and I thought of nothing but the beautiful sounds lifting off from my child's lips. Is it possible that such utterances are all the more beautiful for the battles that lay won beneath them? Surely these words were hard fought. I know it well.

While I sit smiling in the corner chair, my son sings his sentences out loud. Here is newfound confidence; here is surprising joy. I hear it in his voice. I almost laugh aloud with pleasure, imagining his glowing face. He is only a child, but in some profound way, he knows what I know: we're witnessing magic. Science and research and theory and method have taught us well, but this is something else altogether—a mystery of the most beautiful kind. Maybe this is "the human spirit." Or maybe this is faith becoming sight.

Dr. Pierce asks me if I remember his words. *Yes, I remember.* I've hung my hopes on them a thousand times since our early days of vision therapy and reading remediation: *One day, it will all come together. These building blocks that you're working so hard to form will fit together into an organized visual system. And then? He will read.*

How could he have been so sure? *He will read.* What about changing prescriptions and broken glasses and eye muscle surgeries and mom-who-is-tired and little boy fits? *He will read.* What about hours of slow homework and unmemorized verses and poor handwriting and weekly appointments and wandering focus? *He will read.* What if it's too hard? If it takes years? If we miss a step? If I have doubts? If we feel alone? *He will read. One day, Sara—he will read.*

A doctor is not a prophet, and a mother is no savior. But in some mysterious providence, we met one another today to partake in a new joy: *Today, he read.*

Finishing the Long Race

There is something magical about the end of a long-distance race. One of my favorite race trails weaves around wooded hills and valleys before eventually routing runners across a ridgetop and down a steep, winding hill to the finish line. When I am still trotting along the ridgetop, I can hear the echo of the announcer calling out the names of runners who have completed the race. That sound fills me with fresh energy and motivation because I know the end is near; I am close to reaching my goal. Aching muscles and sore feet are thoughts of the past; excitement reigns, and I muster up the strength to accelerate my speed. After barreling down switchbacks in the final descent, I set my gaze toward the finish line and feel my body do its work. One foot strike across the electronic timing pad registers my success. I am met with a finisher's medal, water, and accolades, and I smile at my success. These are the best race days—but not the only ones.

I also recall humbly hobbling across the finish line of one half-marathon in tears, desperate to waddle to my vehicle and wrap myself up in warm, dry clothes. After pulling my hunched frame upright, I swiped the mingling rain, tears, and sweat off my face with the back of my hand and looked at my race partner with a grimace. In a word, I was *miserable*. After running 13.1 miles in a 45-degree rain, I was tired, shivering, and discouraged. The muscles in my legs pulled taut like stretched rubber bands. Certainly, I was not having fun. My sole desire from mile nine onward had been for the race to be over. In fact, I have zero memories of the finish line—no mental images of the medal or the snacks or the music or the crowd. All I know is that I met my goal and finished another race. I drove away exhausted.

All runners hit the finish line in different conditions; this is true for readers as well. For some students, successfully finishing intense training and reaching reading proficiency will come with immediate fulfillment and joy—the crown of victory. Others will hover near exhaustion, feeling that they have clawed and crawled their way toward the finish line with little else to do on the other side but collapse.

Is "Race" a Misnomer?

Each runner at the start line of a long-distance race has a story to tell. Some are running to raise awareness and funds for charity, and some race in memory of a loved one. Cancer survivors run to celebrate life, and friends rally together to celebrate birthdays. Elite athletes run to compete and win; septuagenarians run because they can. Children race because they're finally old enough, and parents race to remember the joy of the run. I've shared purpose with many of these runners, having raced to raise funds for the Leukemia and Lymphoma Society, to build wells with Samaritan's Purse, and to break my own personal records. When I was younger, I sometimes raced to win my age group, but now I mostly race *to finish well*—a goal that grows ever more precious with injury and age.

Goals reflect values—both in running and reading. When we first began our long-term journey of reading training, my goals for my child had more to do with racing the clock. We needed to make up for lost time and create skill where there was struggle. The whole world of academics was shouting to us to "hurry!" If schooling was a competition, we were certainly behind. Only through diligence and productivity in our training would we catch up to the pack. It didn't take long, however, for me to realize that an unnecessary emphasis on speedy lessons was, in fact, *undermining* our progress. Months of teary frustration yielded some wisdom at last: success at reading need not look like age-graded skill level or high scores on words-per-minute achievement tests; we could finish the race at a different pace and a different time and still merit a medal. Success could look like pursuing reading skill in a way that contributes to the formation of a whole person, believing the reading life to be a goal worthy of whatever pace and means necessary. I cannot overstate the importance of this truth: arriving at a *telos* for reading—and education—has significantly shaped both our training and what we perceive to be success.

A Vision of Success

We've already discussed the significance of prior planning for your child to successfully cross the finish line into the reading life.[1] However, a workable plan necessarily requires a clear vision of what it means to succeed. The end goal often dictates the means by which you achieve it. In her book *Rethinking School*, classical educator Susan

1. See chapter 3, "Getting Ready: Developing a Plan That Works."

Wise Bauer includes a chapter entitled "The End Result" that encourages parents to envision the best possible education for their child, much like we did when considering the reading life at the beginning of this book. In a section called "Thinking Backward," Bauer asks the question, "Who do you want this child to *become*?"[2] The point of her words and the thought experiment that follows is twofold: to remind her readers that (1) the end goal of a child's education will direct the process and (2) education is not simply skill production. Education is fundamentally about the formation of a whole person.

Philosophy drives practice—or, as James K. A. Smith notes, "Anthropology shapes pedagogy."[3] *Who we believe a reader to be* acutely affects the path we choose for reading instruction. A classical approach to teaching reading views each struggling student as intrinsically valuable and the reading life as a pathway to human flourishing. It's a path worth pursuing, regardless of the difficulty, because of its ultimate end: the shaping of a human being. If your aim as a reading teacher is simply to create skill where none exists, your student's finish line will mirror the passing score of an achievement test. However, if your goal is to equip your student with skills that enable him to step into the reading life—the fruits of which we have already discussed—then success is something else altogether; it is an invitation to a lifetime of growth.

Portrait of a Reader

What does it mean *to be a reader*, to cross the finish line into the reading life? The most basic definition of a reader is "one who reads"—but that doesn't get us much closer to discerning real meaning. Perhaps it

2. Susan Wise Bauer, *Rethinking School: How to Take Charge of Your Child's Education* (New York: W. W. Norton, 2018), 148.

3. James K. A. Smith, "Pedagogies of Desire: Recontextualizing Christian Higher Education," Faculty lecture delivered at College of the Ozarks, August 2022.

is more helpful for assessing success to ask: *What is reading*? In their book *Teaching Reading*, reading experts Walcutt, Lamport, and Mc-Cracken suggest three definitions of reading: (1) decoding written text, (2) understanding language, and (3) accessing and experiencing the beauty and ideas that are only available in written works.[4] This tripartite description cannot survive as three isolated definitions because each is dependent on another. *Decoding* the phonetic sounds for a given word, sentence, or passage does not necessitate or imply *understanding* of a text. In the same manner, a student may *comprehend* a passage read aloud to him without being able to decode the words for himself. Is this child a reader? What if a student is able to decode the words of a text and understand the meaning of the individual words— does that mean he has access to the world of beauty and knowledge that is to be found in great literature? Walcutt writes,

> [The third definition of reading] requires a new level of thinking about our subject. It is perhaps the least obvious of the three levels of meaning, but it is as essential to a full definition as are the first two. On a level above a mere understanding of language, reading takes us into a world of art and intellect that is accessible only through the printed page and by virtue of the human art of writing.[5]

A student must acquire the skills of decoding and comprehension before she can engage the richness and beauty of literary works for herself. She must learn to separate a main idea of a topic from its details, to skim, and to scan. She will benefit from an understanding of genres and their differences. But one characteristic is conspicuously absent from the

4. Charles Child Walcutt, Joan Lamport, and Glenn McCracken, *Teaching Reading* (New York: Macmillan, 1974), 18–25.
5. Ibid., 21.

above definition: speed. While an overly slow reader may struggle with comprehension of and engagement with a text (due to the time needed to finish a complete thought or section), speed is not a requirement for being a reader. In fact, deep readers are often slow readers! In her book *On Reading Well*, Karen Swallow Prior exhorts slow readers:

> Certainly, some reading material merits a quick read, but habitual skimming is for the mind what a steady diet of fast food is for the body. Speed-reading is not only inferior to deep reading but may bring more harm than benefits: one critic cautions that reading fast is simply a way of "fooling yourself into thinking you're learning something." . . . Don't be discouraged if you read slowly. Thoughtfully engaging with a text takes time. The slowest readers are often the best readers, the ones who get the most meaning out of a work and are affected most deeply by literature.[6]

In other words, crossing the finish line of reading training need not occur at a sprinter's pace! Your student can achieve true skill and proficiency—and be prepared for the reading life—without breaking any speed records. It's worth noting that many standardized reading assessments lean on speed as an indicator of proficiency. Sometimes accommodations can be made based on documented disabilities or differences, and sometimes they can't. Neither is cause for alarm. Simply be aware that a test score may not be the best indicator of your child's success, and don't let the results deter you from celebrating real progress and achievement. If you are in charge of your student's assessment, look for ways your student can demonstrate what she *can* do instead of focusing on what she *can't*. Doing so reframes achievement and gives your student another

---

6. Karen Swallow Prior, *On Reading Well: Finding the Good Life through Great Books* (Grand Rapids: Brazos Press, 2018), 17.

opportunity to observe creative problem-solving at work—something he's likely to need in numerous areas of life. Taking his cues from you, he will learn to harness his responses according to what matters. Remember your goal, and measure your progress accordingly.

When the Finish Line Is Blurry

The finish line is hard to define for some of us. Not every hindrance to reading proficiency can be overcome; some students will spend their entire lives battling physical disabilities, cognitive limitations, or emotional disorders. This book is mostly aimed at parents and teachers of students with mild to moderate disabilities or learning differences, but if your student is experiencing severe limitations, do not despair. Your child is valuable, your work important, and your race can still be run! The unique task ahead of you is to envision the finish line together with your student: How can this child engage the world as a reader? How can he or she experience the fruits of the reading life? Achieving such ends may necessitate the use of assistive technology or a human companion/ aide—and will most certainly require problem solving and creative thought. My encouragement to you is to block out the constraints of the modern educational system, refuse the lie that you are on a time clock, and envision with fresh imagination and hope the possibilities of growth for your student. If the possibilities were limitless, *what would her reading life look like*? Press on toward that end, knowing that whatever you achieve will benefit your child—and bless her community. Yours will be a powerful reminder that "weakness is the way."

Finish Line or Start Line?

After long-term labor, you may be tempted to look towards the "finish line" of your student's long run to reading as an end to the years of energy and effort you have devoted to reading instruction and reme-diation. Indeed, there is reason to celebrate hard-fought progress and achievement—and even reason to assume that your budding reader will no longer need you in quite the same way that he once did. How-ever, it would be a mistake to suggest that there is one final end mark to the journey of the reading life.

In many respects, finishing the period of intense training (in de-coding, comprehension, reading sub-skills, genre orientation…) that you've embarked upon with your child is to usher him across the *start line* of the reading life. Your student now has the tools to pursue read-ing for herself; her growth as a reader has only just begun to blossom. Part of the beauty of the reading life is that it serves us long past our childhood days: "Throwing ourselves into this dance with text has the potential to change us at every stage of our reading lives."[7] My own reading life testifies to this truth: long past primary school reading lessons, I'm still reading new stories and dancing new steps!

Transformed

Last week, I sat down with a child I almost didn't recognize. He ended his school day successfully and bounded into the house, dropping his backpack by the stairs. He called to me as he reached for a snack from the fridge: "Hey mom, after I finish my homework, do you want to read that new book you got me?" Waving away his wishful thinking like an imaginary fly, I chuckled, well aware of how long his home-work would take. I doubted he would have the energy to find the book, much less flip it open to read the first page, after his work was complete. I was mistaken.

7. Maryann Wolf, *Proust and the Squid: The Story and Science of the Reading Brain* (New York: Harper Perennial, 2007), 140.

More than an hour later, I remembered my child's request. Considering the fatigue of a full day of focused visual work, I doubted his resolve: "Still want to read that book, buddy?" He smiled—and promptly ran off in search of the book in question. Moments later, we sat side-by-side on the plush carpet of my bedroom floor, newly acquired text in hand. He read to me not out of obligation—as so many of our reading sessions require—but out of *joy*. He pushed his way through the text with determination and fervor, stopping to check my delight at each new page's revelation. I won't soon forget his sparkling eyes, reaching out to me as if to give a long-saved-up-for gift. It cost him something—to be sure—but he was a cheerful giver, indeed.

That evening, I didn't sit down to read a book *to* my child; I sat down to read *with* him. We shared the joy of words and sentences pointing our thoughts upward, to an imaginary realm. We learned new facts, asked curious questions, and inhabited faraway places together. Wonder reigned and gave birth to lively conversation that hopped and rambled alongside each page. I relished these moments—and remembered when they were only a dream. When the clock registered bedtime, my son marked our place for next time with focused intent. Watching my one-time little boy walk to the door, I marveled at his tremendous growth. Somehow, without conscious recognition, my child had passed into his own reading life.

CH. 7 "NOTES FROM THE TRAINER": A FEW QUESTIONS & ANSWERS FROM DR. DAVID PIERCE, OD

How have you seen different views of a student's "finish line" inform his/her training?

One of my clients was a young girl who had very low vision. Her parents brought her in for an evaluation, hoping to find something that could help her. I almost didn't offer therapy because I didn't know if I could help the child improve. Then I noticed the young girl's hat. I initiated conversation about it and discovered she had crocheted it herself. I realized in a moment that this child could do complex tasks. I had been defaulting to a scientific assessment instead of looking for indications of opportunity. I showed her parents some tools, and they began chipping away at foundational visualization skills.

With diligent effort on the part of the parents, it took this young lady a year and a half to learn her alphabet. Rare is the teacher who would persistently wait this long for progress—but this child's parents did. Years later, I received the student's high school graduation invitation in the mail. At the event, I asked one of the teachers if this young woman could truly read, or if her graduation had been merely ceremonial. The teachers affirmed her skill—accomplishment built through years of labor and effort.

I have little doubt that such parents, at times, feel as if their child might never reach the finish line. This is especially true for those who feel the pressure to reach a certain age-graded skill level in a limited amount of time. The reality is that not all races are run at the same pace. The young woman in this story is no less a reader than a child who learned his alphabet in a matter of weeks or months—yet her journey was quite different.

Do you find speed to be a significant factor in/indicator of reading success? Why/why not?

In short, *no*. Reading speed indicates how quickly a person can process multiple words in one glance. A child can't achieve reading speed until he is confident with each word; fluency is an end-stage result. Fluency is a measure of how well a student can process multiple words at a time. However, a good reader is someone who comprehends and visualizes well. If a child's fluency isn't good, but he has great comprehension, this should not be assessed as reading failure! If a student demonstrates good fluency, but he can't remember the content of a passage, that isn't reading success! Speed (fluency) is only an issue when it interferes with comprehension. I've seen countless readers who can decode and comprehend well, but they will always read slowly. They are slow processors, but they are absolutely readers!

Do you truly see clients with serious visual (or other) limitations overcome them to become readers? What gives you confidence that this endeavor is possible?

... Absolutely, all the time. That's what we do! The kids that have been given up on are the ones we see. Parents visit us after their child has encountered numerous academic obstacles or hasn't responded to any attempted interventions. The ones who aren't successful after seeing us are the ones I remember most—and honestly, those are few and far between. The vast majority of clients who come to my clinic with reading or spelling problems and engage in some form of perceptual therapy *do* find success. Reading does not occur in the eyes; it occurs in the brain—our vision, and our hearing, and our touch, and our speech—they're all well integrated.[8] We must consider the whole system that engages for

---

8. Maryanne Wolf offers a powerful overview of the brain's reading process: "Whenever we name even a single letter, we are activating entire networks of specific neuronal groups in the visual cortex, which correspond to entire networks of equally specific language-based cell groups, which correspond to networks of specific articulatory-motor cell groups—all with millisecond precision." *Reader Come Home: The Reading Brain in a Digital World*, (New York: HarperCollins, 2018), 19-20.

reading. Visual acuity, eye tracking, and eye teaming (both eyes working together) get information to the brain, but where does it go from there? Processing must be addressed in order to find reading progress. Building visualization helps clients say it, write it, think it—that combination forms a strong foundation for reading. I can think of a thousand cases of success. It's the ones who moved away or encountered another impasse that I think about and wonder about their end result

Acknowledgments

This book is born of more than the effort and time it took to write it; its pages reveal a story that has developed over years of struggle. As such, I owe my greatest thanks to those who have supported our family on this long road to reading.

This book would not exist without my son Moses, whose different way of seeing the world has enhanced my own. His diligence and patient labor have modeled a tenacity and discipline that have inspired his parents, teachers, siblings, and friends. It is no exaggeration to say that his struggle to overcome obstacles to the reading life has displayed the power of God to me in the midst of human weakness. For that, I am deeply grateful—and profoundly changed.

The insights in this book have not been gained in isolation. My husband, Rusty, has leaned into this journey alongside me, so often leading and encouraging me when I struggled to find my way. His unique position as my husband, conversation partner, editor, and friend has helped me process ideas, problem-solve, and think creatively about ways to teach all our children. In many ways, he is the silent co-author of this book, having shared every frustration, sorrow, and joy of leading our struggling student into the reading life.

I am also deeply grateful for the skill and care of Dr. David Pierce, who has demonstrated his passion for helping children with vision-related learning problems from the first time we met. His constant encouragement, openness to dialogue, and faithful friendship has supported our family for many years. I'm thankful for his willingness to serve many other families through his contributions to this book.

Dr. Kevin Clark and Cheryl Swope have offered similar encouragement, and I am grateful for their desire to equip parents and teachers of struggling learners in pursuit of an excellent education for any child. Cheryl's work and friendship has often renewed my hope in classically educating children with special needs when the task seems daunting, or even insurmountable.

My parents, Jerry and Shirley Davis, have never wavered in their support of both me and our struggling reader. They have joyfully given not only their love and encouragement, but their time, resources, and even a tutoring space when my son's school was off limits during the COVID-19 pandemic. I am especially grateful for my father's vision for starting School of the Ozarks, the classical Christian school that all four of my children attend.

My children—Sophia, Eleanor, Moses, and Henry—have supported this work with their gifts of time, encouragement, and inspiration. I'm grateful for the privilege of being their mother and, oftentimes, their teacher.

Numerous teachers, colleagues, and friends have also supported this work. I'm grateful for how each one has served to refine ideas, encourage creativity, pray alongside us in the valleys, and celebrate with us on the mountaintops of success.

Finally, I'm grateful for my editors at the CiRCE Institute, who have helped this project come to fruition. I'm thankful for their visible commitment to supporting struggling readers in the classical school and homeschool.